D0629966

every teenager's
little black book
special gift edition

by blaine bartel

Harrison House
Tulsa, Oklahoma

10 09 08 07   10 9 8 7 6 5 4 3 2 1

every teenager's little black book special gift edition
ISBN 13: 978-1-57794-908-4
ISBN 10: 1-57794-908-0
Copyright © 2007 by Blaine Bartel
P.O. Box 691923
Tulsa, Oklahoma 74179

Published by Harrison House, Inc.
P.O. Box 35035
Tulsa, Oklahoma 74153

contents

little black book on cool   1

little black book on sex and dating   57

little black book on reaching your dreams   119

little black book of hard to find information   191

every teenager's
little black book
on cool

3 REASONS WHY COOL DOESN'T TRY—IT IS

Truly cool people don't have to work at it—they just are. Let's be honest: if you have to try to be cool, you probably won't have a lot of people looking up to you. Let's check out 3 reasons why cool doesn't have to try.

1. **Being cool is an honor that only others can bestow upon you.** Remember, the Bible's counterparts for the modern word *cool* are *favored* and *accepted*. Only God and people can show you favor and acceptance.

2. **Truly cool people focus on others, not on themselves.** Matthew 23:12 says that those who humble themselves will be exalted.

3. **Most cool people don't even realize they are cool.** They're too busy making a difference in their world.

4 THINGS THAT ARE DEFINITELY NOT COOL

Have you ever had someone at school try to impress you in some way? They were thinking, *Wow! Am I ever cool!* And you were thinking, *When is this person going to get a clue?* Once again, cool people don't have to work to impress you. Here are 4 things that are definitely not cool.

1. You are not cool when you talk about yourself most of the time. The Bible says, "Let another man praise you, and not your own mouth" (Prov. 27:2 NKJV).

2. You are not cool because of how you walk or what you wear. You are accepted and favored because of the good person you are, not the perception you try to create.

3. It is definitely not cool to live a life of sin and personal pleasure. The Word of God warns us, "The way of transgressors is hard" (Prov. 13:15).

4. It is not cool to make others feel small by putting them down with your words. Remember the law of

sowing and reaping—if you sow encouragement, you'll reap it back.

5 WAYS TO KNOW YOU AREN'T COOL

Maybe you're reading this little book right now and you're still not sure: *Am I cool?* So I want to help you with some important identification marks of people who will not gain favor with others. Here are 5 ways to know you aren't cool.

1. If you constantly live in self-pity, looking to get attention, you are not cool.

2. If you try to impress people with your money, possessions, or accomplishments, you are not cool.

3. If you are sharp-tongued, gossipy, and critical of others, you are not cool.

4. If you only treat people you like and know with love and respect, you are not cool.

5. If you spend the majority of the time thinking about yourself, having little regard for Christ and others, you are not cool.

4 REASONS YOU SHOULD BE COOL

God wants you to be cool, accepted, and favored. The Scripture says, "Let not mercy and truth forsake you; bind them around your neck, write them on the tablet of your heart, and so find favor and high esteem in the sight of God and man" (Prov. 3:3,4 NKJV). You can enjoy favor, acceptance, and popularity with both God and people. Here are 4 reasons why you should be cool.

1. Cool, accepted people have the ability to influence others for good. That includes a witness of your Christian faith.

2. Cool, favored people have confidence to do things others believe to be impossible or improbable.

3. Accepted people find it easy and natural to show others God's love and acceptance.

4. Cool people stand up for truth and don't need everyone to agree with them or even like them.

6 WAYS ANY PERSON CAN BECOME COOL

Let's get right to the point: you want to be accepted and popular with people. Who doesn't? Now, you know you can't try to gain popularity and "coolness" the way the world tries to manufacture it. So how does a person become "Christ-like cool"?

1. You become cool when you stand up for what is right and don't care who stands with you.

2. You become cool when you reach out to the poor, the hurting, the lost—those who are "uncool."

3. You become cool when you take time for those whom many overlook—children. God loves kids, and so should we.

4. You become cool when you freely admit your short-comings, pick up where you've failed, and move forward with godly confidence.

5. You become cool when you put God first in your words, your actions, and your plans.

6. You become cool when you could care less about being cool.

[COOL CONFIDENCE]

4 DIFFERENCES BETWEEN
CONFIDENCE AND ARROGANCE

Some people think that confidence is pride. You can be confident and very humble. Pride is confidence in the wrong things. True confidence comes from a solid foundation of knowing who you are in Christ. Look at these 4 differences between confidence and arrogance and check up on yourself.

1. Confidence is security in who we are in Christ. Arrogance is self-reliance because of what we have, who we know, or what we have done.

2. Confidence is knowing that "we can do all things through Christ Jesus" versus trusting what we can do ourselves. (Phil. 4:13.)

3. Confidence is knowing our past is forgiven by God and we are in good standing with Him by faith. Arrogance is confidence in our works and our righteousness. (Eph. 2:8.)

4. Confidence is knowing that God is on our side and, therefore, it doesn't matter who is against us.

Arrogance is security from circumstances and our own resources. (Rom. 8:31.)

Be confident because of who you are in Christ Jesus. With Him on your side, you can't fail.

5 MARKS OF A CONFIDENT PERSON

Use this as a check to see if you are confident in who you are in Christ.

1. You aren't afraid to meet new people.

2. You like to try new things and see new places.

3. You aren't afraid to take calculated risks in order to achieve something you want.

4. You don't get discouraged and depressed when you fail. Instead, you pick yourself back up.

5. It doesn't bother you much when people criticize you.

If all of the statements above describe you, you are very confident. If 4 of the statements are true about you, your confidence is solid and improving. Three true statements means you could use some improvement. It's not looking good if only 2 statements are true; you are limiting yourself from great experiences. If you only found 1 statement to be true, reread this book every day until all the statements are true.

Remember, in Christ you are a new creation. (2 Cor. 5:17.)

3 MUSTS FOR BUILDING REAL CONFIDENCE

If you need more confidence in your life, here is a simple
game plan that will help you grow.

1. **Find your identity in Christ Jesus.** If we look to
   ourselves for confidence, we have many reasons to be
   insecure and disappointed. But in Christ, we are
   amazing. Look up these Scriptures: 2 Corinthians
   5:17; Philippians 4:13; Colossians 1:22; Jude 24;
   Romans 8:15.

2. **Surround yourself with people who believe in
   you.** Small people criticize big dreams. Don't allow
   your faith and self-esteem to be robbed by critical and
   negative people. Surround yourself with people who
   believe in you.

3. **Take small steps to build big victories.** We all
   have things in our lives we are secretly afraid of.
   Maybe it's heights, meeting new people, trying new
   foods, or sharing our faith. Don't take a leap of faith;
   take little steps toward overcoming your fears. The

Bible says, "The steps of a good man are ordered by the Lord" (Ps. 37:23).

Build these 3 steps to confidence into your daily routine, and watch your confidence soar.

6 ENEMIES THAT WILL TRY
TO STEAL YOUR CONFIDENCE

In battle, one of the best advantages you can have is to understand your enemy. The more you know your enemy, the better you can avoid his traps and attacks. Here are 6 enemies that will try to steal your confidence.

1. **Negative people who criticize you.** You get to choose who your friends are. If your friends pull you down, get new friends.

2. **Unconfessed sin.** This will rob your confidence before God. Don't be like Adam and Eve who hid from God. Go to Him, confess it, and be forgiven. (1 John 1:9.)

3. **Listening to your feelings rather than God's Word.** Feelings will betray you because they are subject to your circumstances. Fix your eyes on God's unchanging Word.

4. **Looking at your past to determine your future.** You may have a past littered with failure, but that

doesn't mean you can't succeed. A righteous person falls 7 times but keeps getting back up. (Prov. 24:16.)

5. **Looking at the problem rather than God's promise for the solution.** God's Word has a promise for any problem you face.

6. **Comparing yourself to other people.** You are a great you but a lousy anyone else. Be you. You are great. (Jer. 1:5, 29:11; Ps. 138:8, 139.)

Don't let the enemy steal your confidence. You have every reason to be secure. You're on God's team, and we win.

7 SCRIPTURES THAT PROVE GOD IS CONFIDENT IN YOU

Here are 7 encouraging Scriptures to look up and commit to memory.

1. **Psalm 138:8:** God will fulfill His purpose for your life.

2. **John 3:16:** God believed in you enough to allow His Son, Jesus, to die for you.

3. **Mark 16:15:** After Jesus rose from the dead, He gave His ministry to His disciples and us to finish.

4. **Jude 24:** He said He will keep you from falling and present you in His presence with great joy.

5. **Acts 1:8:** He gave us His power and Holy Spirit to witness.

6. **John 15:16:** He handpicked you. You're His first-round draft pick.

7. **Ephesians 2:5:** Even while we were lost, He made us alive with Him.

If God is confident in you, that should be enough for you. He is the Creator of the universe, and He is on your side. You can't lose.

[FINDING FAVOR]

4 STEPS TO FINDING FAVOR WITH GOD

Let's be honest. If you can get yourself in favor with the most powerful Person in the universe, you're going to do really well. The great thing is that God has told us clearly in His Word that we can fall into favor with Him. Here are 5 steps to getting there.

1. **Diligently seek after Him.** He promises to reward and bless anyone who wholeheartedly seeks Him. (Heb. 11:6.)

2. **Search out the wisdom of God's Word.** He promises that when we discover His wisdom we will obtain favor from Him. (Prov. 8:35.)

3. **Develop a lifestyle of praising God without apology.** The churches in the book of Acts were bold to praise God with their voices and found favor with all the people. (Acts 2:47.)

4. **Walk into goodness and integrity towards others.** God promises you favor, but condemns the person who is wicked in one's actions. (Prov. 12:2.)

4 STEPS TO FINDING FAVOR WITH FRIENDS

Everyone wants to have good friends. In order to have a good friend, you must learn to be one. There are very real reasons why everyone seems to like some people, while others are constantly rejected. Here are 4 practical steps to finding good friends.

1. **Break out of your shell of fear.** Don't wait for people to reach out to you. Be bold to say hello to people and make conversation.

2. **Give friends their space.** Don't monopolize people's time or constantly follow them around. When you begin to smother people with attention, they will naturally want to avoid you.

3. **Be confident in yourself and your abilities.** If you are constantly putting yourself down and wallowing in self-pity, people will tire of you soon.

4. **Have a giving heart without trying to "buy" your friendships.** Be generous and thoughtful

without feeling like you have to do things to keep a certain friend. If you have to buy or give someone something all the time, the person is probably not a friend anyway.

3 STEPS TO FINDING FAVOR
WITH THE OPPOSITE SEX

There is something that happens when you move into your
teenage years. All of a sudden, you're not as concerned about
"girls' germs" or "boys' germs" as you were when you were 7
or 8. During your teens, God slowly prepares you to someday
enter into the covenant of marriage. It is important that you
learn how to properly treat and respect the opposite sex, since
you will eventually live with one of them forever. Here are 3
simple steps to remember.

1. **Learn how to pass on sincere compliments
   about their character and accomplishments.**
   Make them feel appreciated for who they are and what
   they've worked hard to achieve.

2. **Be nice to all.** Don't become "a snob" or "stuck up"
   because you only associate with those who are good-
   looking or popular. Remember, Jesus died and shed
   His blood for every person, not just the ones He liked.

3. **Show respect and purity physically.** Your body
   belongs to you. Other people's bodies belong to them.

The only time this changes is when 2 people are married. So, until that time comes for you, stay clear of tempting situations. (1 Cor. 7:1-4.)

6 STEPS TO FINDING FAVOR
IN THE WORKPLACE

God wants to help you succeed in all your work. Your success in your job and career will be a direct result of your ability to get along with people. One of the coolest things in the world is having a job you love and working with people you really like. Here are 6 steps to get you there.

1. Don't treat your boss one way and everyone else a different way. People will see your hypocrisy and resent you.

2. Never cheat your company or business by stealing. I'm not just talking about their products or supplies; this also includes their time. If you're constantly late to work, taking long breaks, or leaving early, it's like stealing money out of the cash register, because "Time is money."

3. Don't try to destroy someone at your work in order to get that person's position for yourself. It will eventually backfire, and you'll be out!

4. When someone else does a good job at your work, compliment the person personally and in front of your boss.

5. Never try to take authority or leadership that hasn't been given to you. Just do your job, and stay out of business that isn't yours.

6. Always give 100 percent. If you can give 110 percent, you were never giving 100 percent in the first place!

3 STEPS TO FINDING FAVOR
WITH YOUR PARENTS

One of the coolest things in life is enjoying a happy home.
You can learn to become a source of joy in your family. I've
got 3 teenage boys who everyone at school and church thinks
are really "cool." But they are also great guys at home. The
rebel attitude is not cool. In fact, it will cause you some very
"uncool" moments in life. Here are 3 things you can do to
ensure a great time at home.

1. **Choose to obey your parents immediately,
   whether you feel like it or not.** You're eventually
   going to have to do it—right? So just get it done and
   out of the way.

2. **Honor your parents when you speak to them.**
   Even if you don't agree with them and want to discuss
   something or negotiate a "better deal," do it without
   the anger and the attitude. You'll be amazed at the
   results!

3. **Be truthful, even when it gets you in trouble.**

   You lose favor quickly when you cannot be trusted. It
   is better to take the heat if you have it coming, than to
   lie and avoid it. Lies are eventually uncovered, and the
   consequences are much more damaging than telling
   the truth would have been.

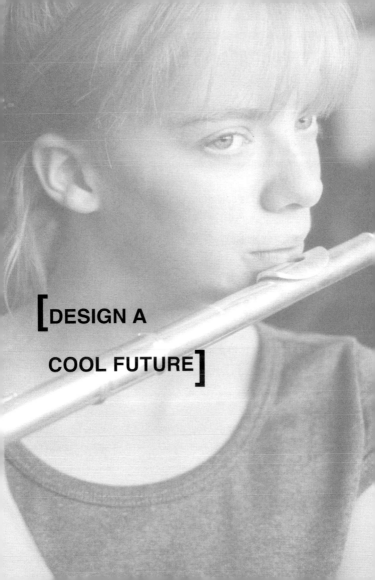

[DESIGN A

COOL FUTURE]

7 ABSOLUTES OF GOD'S WILL FOR YOUR LIFE

Have you ever heard someone say, "God moves in mysterious ways"? I sure am glad that statement isn't true. The will of God doesn't have to be mysterious. Here are 7 things you can absolutely count on.

1. **God's will is salvation.** Our heavenly Father desires that all of humankind have eternal life with Him. That includes you.

2. **God's will is dominion.** Dominion simply means control. God wants you to apply His Word and take control of your body, thought life, attitude, and future.

3. **God's will is discipleship.** We are to grow in our walk with Christ. As we mature, we are to help others do the same.

4. **God's will is unity.** Your words and actions must be united with God's Word.

5. **God's will is stewardship.** We are to take proper care of our time, money, abilities, and all God has entrusted us with.

6. **God's will is relationships.** Through the power of relationships, you will be able to accomplish things that would be impossible if you were alone.

7. **God's will is progressive.** God has a plan for your life that will be completed one step at a time, not in leaps or bounds.

4 WAYS GOD GIVES YOU DIRECTION

Do you need direction? Good, because God wants to give it to you. The direction of God is not hard to come by. Here are 4 ways He will give it to you.

1. **The Word (Bible):** the most practical way that God gives direction. All other ways must line up with this way.

2. **Peace:** how God will lead you. His peace will be deep down inside letting you know you're headed in the right direction.

3. **People:** pastors, teachers, parents, and friends. God will speak through these people whom He has strategically placed in your life.

4. **Desires:** what you want to do. Do you like making art, building, or helping others? God has placed desires in your heart to help give you direction.

5 DECISIONS YOUNG PEOPLE MAKE
THAT SABOTAGE THEIR FUTURE

Who you are now and who you will be is determined by the decisions you make. One out of every one person will make decisions. When you have to make a decision and don't, that is in itself a decision. So the question is what kind of decision-maker are you going to be? To help keep you from sabotaging your future, here are 5 decisions *not* to make.

1. **Disobey your parents.** God has placed your parents in your life to help guide you.

2. **Make quick decisions.** Before making a decision, take time to think it over.

3. **Develop wrong relationships.** The people you spend time with probably have the most influence on the decisions you make.

4. **Wait for your big break.** You must get off the couch and pursue your God-given destiny.

5. **Give up.** Both winners and losers face challenges, but winners don't quit.

6 STEPS TO FINDING YOUR HUSBAND OR WIFE

Finding that special person God has for you is one of the most important journeys you will take. Here are 6 steps to help you in your search.

1. **Prepare.** Be sure you are ready emotionally and, most importantly, spiritually.

2. **Ask.** Pray for guidance in finding your spouse. Remember: you have not because you ask not. (James 4:2.)

3. **Obey**. Obedience to God's Word will keep you on the right track.

4. **Focus.** Keep your eyes and heart on Jesus, not the anxiety of searching.

5. **Wait.** Be patient and understand that God has a perfect time for your paths to cross.

6. **Relax.** As you are doing your part, God will take care of the rest.

3 KEYS TO EFFECTIVE PLANNING

If you want success, you must plan for it. Someone once asked Wayne Gretzky how he became the best goal scorer in the history of hockey. He replied, "While everyone else is chasing the puck, I go to where the puck is going to be." He planned ahead. Let's take a look at 3 keys to effective planning.

1. **Prayer.** You may not know what the future holds, but God does. God promises that if you will ask Him, He will show you things that you could never figure out on your own. (Jer. 33:3.)

2. **Goal setting.** Write out exactly what it is you are planning for. You will be amazed how this key will unlock your future.

3. **Prioritizing.** You can't keep your priorities if you don't have any. Putting things in order will help you plan for and accomplish the most important things first.

[COOL, HARD CASH]

3 REASONS IT IS COOL TO MAKE GOOD MONEY

In the past, some Christians have believed and taught that all Christians should be poor. Sadly, they have had a very poor understanding of what God says in the Bible. While the Lord is opposed to us making money our god and primary focus, He wants to bring finances into our hands for the right purposes. Check out 3 reasons why making good money is cool with Him.

1. God wants you to learn how to provide well for yourself and your family. In fact, He says that if you don't make money and provide for your home, you are worse than an infidel (a really bad sinner)! (1 Tim. 5:8.)

2. God wants you to use your money to sow into His kingdom in order to make provision to take the message of Christ around the world. It costs money to print Bibles, support missionaries, and build soul-winning churches. (2 Cor. 9:6-11.)

3. Simply, God loves His children. As a Father, He wants to meet all of our needs and even our desires. As long

as we keep our eyes and hearts focused on Him, it is His will to bless us abundantly. (Ps. 37:4; Matt. 6:33; Phil. 4:19.)

5 WAYS TO GET A GREAT JOB

I've held a job since I was 12 years old. I've learned how to work hard and have never, ever been fired. I've discovered that if you give your best, you will have the opportunity to eventually do work that you enjoy and get promoted into a really cool job. Here are 5 ways to land a great job or career.

1. Get out into the workplace and hunt your job down. Knock on doors, set up interviews, and learn to sell your desire and ability.

2. Be sure you have properly trained and prepared yourself for the job you really want. If it means college, find a way to get to college. Read, learn, intern, volunteer, and do whatever it takes to become the best in your field.

3. Start out in any company or organization being willing to do the small things that other "big shots" aren't willing to do. It will separate and distinguish you from the pack.

4. Set your sights high. Don't allow your own self-doubt or other people's lack of support to stop you from going after your goals. (Mark 11:24.)

5. Pray and trust God to open up the doors supernaturally. He can, and He will. (Jer. 33:3.)

3 KINDS OF GIVING EVERY PERSON OUGHT TO DO

One of the unbreakable laws of the universe is the law of sowing and reaping, seedtime and harvest. (Gen. 8:22.) It usually doesn't feel like it at the time, but when you give your money into the ground of good works, it will produce and come back to you multiplied many times over. Here are 5 kinds of "money-seed" you should sow, expecting God to bring a harvest back to you.

1.   Sow the tithe into your local church. A tithe is one-tenth of what you earn, and we are commanded in Scripture to give into the "storehouse," or where we receive our primary spiritual food—our church. (Mal. 3:10.)

2.   Sow special offerings or gifts into ministries that are reaching people and to other worthy causes that are truly impacting people. (Phil. 4:15-19.)

3.   Sow into the lives of those who are poor and unable to provide for themselves. (Prov. 22:9.) Keep your gift as

private as possible so as not to humiliate the one who receives it.

4 THINGS COOL PEOPLE LEARN
TO BUY THE RIGHT WAY

In life, you are going to do a lot of spending. I believe it is important to be a good steward of the money God gives by being wise in the way we purchase things. It is completely "uncool" to waste our money on things that don't last or are unhealthy or unproductive. Now for the things you must learn to buy right.

1. **Luxuries.** This is the stuff you really don't "need" but would be cool to have. A couple of points to remember: don't make impulsive purchases; allow a cooling-off period before you pull the trigger; never put a luxury on credit—pay cash; allow luxury purchases in proper proportion to your budget for the rest of your expenses.

2. **Vehicle.** This is the big-ticket item. When starting out, don't buy a brand-new one. You'll lose a few thousand dollars the minute you drive it off the lot. Be careful as you search for a good used vehicle. Compare prices, get the vehicle checked by an

independent mechanic, and make sure you can afford the payments if you finance it.

3. **Food.** Stay away from a lot of junk. Learn to eat healthy!

4. **Clothes.** Cheap clothes are tempting, but they often don't last or look very good. Spend a little extra to get something sharp.

5. **House.** It's probably a little way down the road for you right now, but don't allow yourself to have a "renter's mentality." The quicker you can buy your own place, even if it's a "fixer-upper," the better! Get wise counsel from those who have purchased several homes successfully.

3 INVESTMENTS ANY TEENAGER SHOULD START RIGHT NOW

One of the coolest things is to see a young person who has learned early on the discipline of setting money aside for the future. Early financial investment will bring great rewards. If a parent put $1000 a year into an investment that reaps 10 percent for just the first 10 years of a child's life, when that child reached 60, there would be more than $1 million from that $1000 investment. The point is to start doing something now. Here are 3 ideas:

1. Go to your parents' bank, open a savings account, and commit to put a certain amount in it every month.

2. Save up your money to buy shares of stock in a strong American company, such as Wal-Mart, GE, and others that you know will be around a long time. Then leave it! Forget it's even there, and in about 20 or 30 years you'll be amazed at how it grows!

3. Once you get a regular job, commit to put at least 10 percent of your income each month into savings,

stocks, or mutual funds. If you need wisdom and help as to how to do this most effectively, talk to a financial counselor at your bank or someone in your church who is financially successful.

[THE UNSELFISH LIFE]

4 REASONS PEOPLE BECOME SELFISH

Have you ever wondered how someone could be so selfish? To answer that question and to help you avoid that same pitfall, here is a list of 4 reasons why people become selfish.

1. **They make the choice to be selfish.** We must make a decision not to be selfish, even if we don't feel like it. I have found that as you act on your decision, the feelings will come.

2. **They take for granted the joy of giving.** Not only will an unselfish act bring joy to others, but the giver will receive joy as well.

3. **They have unrenewed thinking.** We're all born naturally selfish, but that doesn't mean we must stay that way. We need to put selfless thoughts in and selfish thoughts out.

4. **They're unthankful.** Unthankfulness will cause people to become selfish. People who are unthankful stop recognizing the goodness of others; therefore, they develop an unwillingness to give.

5 UNSELFISH ACTS IN THE BIBLE

Do you need a role model of unselfishness? The stories of the Bible have been placed there for our example. Let's take a look at 5 unselfish acts we can imitate.

1. **Abraham and Isaac. (Gen. 22.)** Abraham was willing to give his beloved son for the cause of God.

2. **The crucifixion of Christ. (Matt. 27.)** Jesus Christ, being without sin, died the death of a criminal so that we could live a life free from sin.

3. **Joseph and his brothers. (Gen. 37-45.)** Joseph did not strike back in vengeance towards his brothers, who sold him into slavery, when he had the opportunity to do so.

4. **The poor widow. (Luke 21:1-4.)** Although poor, this widow gave all she could give.

5. **The Good Samaritan. (Luke 10:30-36.)** This Samaritan acted unselfishly, regardless of what others might have thought.

5 SCRIPTURES THAT FOCUS ON GIVING

Every day you will have a choice whether to give or not to give. Whether your little brother wants to borrow something or a crazy friend wants you to shave his back hair, here for your encouragement are 5 Scriptures on giving.

1. **Luke 6:38:** Giving not only blesses the receiver, but also the giver.

2. **Proverbs 21:26:** As the righteousness of God, we are not to be stingy in our giving.

3. **2 Corinthians 9:7:** Be sure your heart is in the right place while giving.

4. **Matthew 10:8:** God has blessed us so that we may bless others.

5. **Acts 20:35:** The giver is better off than the one who receives.

6 PRACTICAL ACTIONS OF
LOVE TOWARDS OTHERS

God is love, and as imitators of Christ we are to illuminate His love towards others. Maybe you need some advice to get started. Here are some potential actions to get the ball rolling.

1. **Be polite.** Treat others with respect. Say please and thank you. Also remember, guys: ladies first.

2. **Smile.** Show off those pearly whites. This small gesture will go a long way.

3. **Share.** This unselfish act is packed with power.

4. **Listen.** Give others your full attention. They will appreciate the investment.

5. **Lend a hand.** Mow the lawn for an elderly neighbor, or send a card to a relative you have been praying for.

6. **Give a gift.** There doesn't have to be a special reason, but the best reason of all is to simply say, "I love you."

3 REASONS GIVERS FIND UNUSUAL FAVOR

Favor can bring you before the right people and set up the right circumstances. Wouldn't you like to have favor? As a giver, you can. Here's why:

1. **It's a spiritual law.** As you give, it is as if you are making deposits into a favor bank account that you can withdraw at any time. (Luke 6:38.)

2. **People like givers.** As you give, you become a giant magnet for unusual favor. Don't you enjoy being around givers? I thought so.

3. **God is on your side.** As you are obedient to God's Word, God will open up doors of favor in your life.

every teenager's
little black book
on sex and dating

[DEFINING DATING]

3 THINGS DATING IS NOT

Dating is not really a biblical word at all. That doesn't mean it's wrong to go out with someone on a "date." But it is important to remember what the Bible has to say about developing romantic friendships. If you begin dating without some clear guidelines and boundaries, you are headed for disaster.

Let's start by taking a quick glance at what dating is not.

1. **Dating is not for those who aren't ready.** In my opinion, dating shouldn't even be a consideration until a young person is at least 16 years old. That's been "the law" with my 3 teenage boys, and they're doing just fine with it. That doesn't mean you can't have good friendships with the opposite sex; just keep things in a group environment.

2. **Dating is not a great way to "really get to know someone."** Why? Because everyone is on best behavior during a date. If you really want to get to know someone, watch the person at school every day, or both of you get a job together at McDonald's. Eight straight hours over a hot greaser full of fries will tell you the real tale.

3. **Dating is not all it's cracked up to be.** Think about 2 people out together who hardly know each other. They're young and have limited social skills. They have to try to create awkward conversation for hours on end. The point is, it's usually a whole lot easier to get to know someone among a group of other friends who can help fill those awkward moments, keeping things fun.

3 WAYS CHRISTIAN DATING IS DIFFERENT

The world's idea of dating is dangerous at best. That's why the Scripture tells us not to be conformed to this world, but to be transformed by the renewing of our minds. (Rom. 12:2.) We renew our minds with the knowledge of God's Word.

Here are 3 ways a Christian dating experience should be different from one in the world.

1. In the world, people date to check someone out; a Christian date is focused on building someone up. Dating in the world is like "trying someone on" like a pair of shoes—if they don't fit quite right for you, just disregard them and move on to someone else. A Christian's focus should be on encouraging each other in life and in one another's walk with God.

2. The world bases a large part of success in their dates on connecting physically, while Christians should be prizing spiritual things first. It's not that you shouldn't be attracted to someone by looks, but maintaining sexual purity must be at the top of your commitment to each other.

3. The world will often lie and deceive to achieve their goals in dating. Christians are to be committed to integrity and honesty. Don't try to be someone you are not. Tell the truth. If someone doesn't like the "real you," don't worry about it. Obviously, that person isn't "the one."

3 UNCOMMON THINGS
EVERY GIRL WANTS IN A GUY

King Solomon said that a good man is 1 in 1000 and a good woman is nearly impossible to find. (Eccl. 7:28.) So guys, if you want to be that 1 in 1000, you can separate yourself from the pack by living up to these 3 uncommon characteristics.

1. **A spirit of desire.** Proverbs 21:25 says that the desire of a lazy man kills him. Girls are looking for young men who have vision, drive, and desire for life and are willing to work to reach their goals.

2. **A spirit of kindness.** Proverbs 19:22 tells us that kindness is what is desired in a good man. Learn proper etiquette and manners in the way you should treat people.

3. **A spirit of justice.** A just person is someone who has learned to distinguish right from wrong and is not afraid to stand up for truth. Don't back down to the pressure of friends to do wrong or compromise. Have some backbone and be counted.

3 UNCOMMON THINGS
EVERY GUY WANTS IN A GIRL

All right, ladies, turnabout is fair play. You have some expectations too. In a world that has become increasingly corrupt and vulgar, you can stand above the crowd by the way you choose to live. Anyone can follow the masses, but it will be the few who do the right thing who are exalted, promoted, and blessed with the best relationships and a bright future.

What does a real man want in a girl?

1. **Devotion.** A real man will chase a girl who chases after God and is unwilling to compromise and give in to the world. Be devoted to Christ and devoted to His plans for your life. Guys will follow!

2. **Wisdom.** Knowledge is the acquiring of facts and information. Wisdom knows what direction to go with those facts and information. Guys search for a young woman who has the ability to discern and make good decisions.

3. **Encouragement.** Throughout the Bible, we are instructed to encourage one another, inspiring others with our words and good works. Learn to build people

up, not tear them down. A man needs a woman who believes in him and will be a regular source of strength and encouragement.

4 SIGNS THAT YOU
MAY NOT BE READY TO DATE

Okay, you are at a new stage in your life. You have this attraction to the opposite sex that just wasn't there when you were 7 years old and still playing on the swing set in the backyard. Just because you have this new desire for romance doesn't mean it's time to date. Navigating through the complicated world of boy-girl relationships is like learning to fly a 747 jet. You need lots of instruction, preparation, and maturity before you try to take off.

Here are 4 signs that you may want to wait a while before you get your engines going.

1. **Your parents feel you are too young.** Unless you are out of the house, 27 years old, and have a mom and dad who just can't let go, listen to them. They have been down the road you're on.

2. **You have a significant problem with lust.** If you are struggling with pornography and lack control in your thought life, conquer this area first. (2 Tim. 2:21-22.)

3. **God is not first in your life and priorities.** A strong commitment to Christ is the foundation for any good relationship.

4. **You believe dating will finally make you happy and fulfilled.** People are not your answer. If you look to them for your hope and fulfillment, they can quickly become another one of your problems. Only Jesus Christ can fill you with a love that will take away that empty void.

[FRIENDSHIP BEFORE ROMANCE]

5 WAYS TO ATTRACT NEW FRIENDS

Lee Iacocca says, "Success comes not from what you know, but from who you know and how you present yourself to each of those people."[1] Good friendships are vital to success. Maybe you are in need of some good friends.

Here are 5 ways to attract new friends.

1. **Smile.** Turn that frown upside down. This gesture may be small, but it packs a powerful punch. Showing those pearly whites is a magnet to new friends (be sure those pearls are white). (Prov. 18:24.)

2. **Listen.** Let others talk about themselves, then respond. When someone else is talking, don't be thinking about what you're going to say. Give the person your ear and thoughts. (Prov. 17:28.)

3. **Be dependable.** Be there for others during the good and the bad. Anyone can be there for the fun times, but only a friend will be there when things get rough.

4. **Keep your word.** If you say you are going to do something, do it. Keep your word even if you don't feel like it. If you can't keep a promise, then don't

make it. It's better to under-promise and overachieve. (Prov. 11:3.)

5. **Help others succeed.** Be others-minded. Ask yourself, "How can I help this person?" Then do something about it. If you have this mindset, you will attract so many friends you won't know what to do.

3 FRIENDSHIP KILLERS YOU MUST AVOID

Good friends are hard to come by, and acquiring good friends is only half the battle. The other half is keeping them. If you want to keep your friends, I suggest you don't do these friendship killers.

1. **Gossip.** Gossip is simply mischievous talk about the affairs of others. Proverbs 16:28 says that a gossip separates close friends. A good friend will keep what he or she knows in confidence, unless someone in authority needs to be notified.

2. **Selfishness.** How can we expect to keep the company of others if we are only concerned about ourselves? In Philippians 2:3, Paul wrote that we are to consider others better than ourselves. If we act unselfishly, we will encourage our friendships to grow.

3. **Unforgiveness.** Our friends will make mistakes. Why? Because they are human. As our friends miss it and then turn from their mistakes or sin, we are to forgive them. We are to forgive our friends as Christ forgave us. (Eph. 4:31,32.)

5 THINGS REAL FRIENDS
NEVER DO TO EACH OTHER

If you want to be a real friend, I suggest you do the complete opposite of these 5 things.

1. **Lie and deceive.** A real friend looks out for the interest of others. We must realize that to lie and deceive does not protect anyone, but it hurts all parties involved. Be a person of truth and honesty.

2. **Spread rumors.** Be sure you are a positive promoter for your friends, not a negative rumor spreader. If you're talking bad about someone else, someone else is probably talking bad about you.

3. **Be jealous.** Love is not jealous. (1 Cor. 13:4.) We should be the happiest people our friends know when they succeed. If your friend gets a new video game system, don't be jealous. Enjoy the benefits of your friendship.

4. **Discourage.** Discouragement is simply the taking away of courage. Encourage—give your friends the

courage to face all opportunities and obstacles that come their way. Be your friend's number-one fan.

5. **Give up.** Jesus is our ultimate example of a real friend. Are you thankful He never gave up on us? As a real friend, you shouldn't quit on your friends because of challenging times. Jesus said He would never leave us or forsake us. Let's make that commitment as well.

3 REASONS FRIENDSHIP IS
MORE IMPORTANT THAN ROMANCE

Romance is a good thing. As a married man, I know. However, *friendship* is more important: it should be the foundation that romance is built on. Let's take a look at 3 reasons friendship is more important than romance.

1. **Longevity.** Friendship is long-lasting. Romance is temporary. Romance is defined as a strong, usually short-lived, attachment or feeling. Friendship is there for the long haul.

2. **Not a feeling.** It's a fact. The feeling of romance will come and go. Romance has a lot to do with its environment and circumstances. Friendship, on the other hand, is there whether we feel it or not.

3. **You can be yourself.** You don't have to worry about impressing others. There is no need for you to present yourself in an unrealistic manner to gain affection. A true friend will still love you when you've had one too many Big Macs.

6 FRIENDS THAT ARE NOT
TRUE FRIENDS AT ALL

We have all been in relationships in which we thought someone was our friend and then down the road realized he or she wasn't a true friend. A true friend doesn't just call themself a friend, but backs up his or her words with action. Here are 6 "friends" to avoid.

1. **The back-stabber.** This is someone who acts one way in front of you, but acts totally different behind your back. A back-stabber cannot be trusted by anyone.

2. **The user.** The user is just looking for a temporary friend. This person will borrow your friendship for personal gain and then toss you like a dirty dishrag.

3. **The control freak.** "It's my way or the highway," this one will say. The control freak will not compromise. You're only going and doing what this person wants to do. Your opinion doesn't matter.

4. **The manipulator.** If you don't want to do what the manipulator wants you to do, this person will find a way to convince you to do it his or her way. The

manipulator is sly and will influence you to do things you never thought you would do—all for his or her own selfish ambitions.

5. **The moocher.** This person wants you to provide for his or her every need. "Can I borrow your clothes?" "Can I borrow your car?" "Can I borrow a couple of bucks?" As you give, you'll never receive anything in return. In plain English, this person is a bum.

6. **The complainer.** You can never please the complainer no matter what you do. If you gave this person a $100 bill, he or she would complain because it's not 2 $50 bills. Save yourself and avoid this one.

[BEING THE

RIGHT PERSON]

5 KEY CHARACTERISTICS
OF THE RIGHT PERSON

Are you the right person? Are you the man for the job? Are you the woman who will not compromise? We all want that right job, car, spouse, future, or opportunity. For those things to come our way, each of us must first be the right person.

You can begin now to develop these 5 key characteristics of the right person.

1. Integrity is one of the most important characteristics that anyone could have. The right person is the same no matter whom one is with, what one is doing, or where one is. Image is not everything; integrity is. In the end, your life is about being, not appearing.

2. The second key characteristic of the right person is humility. Proverbs 16:18 NIV says, "Pride goes before destruction, a haughty spirit before a fall." You cannot live a life of destruction and expect to be or find the right person. So humble yourself under God's Word by honoring and obeying His direction.

3. Everyone should have an ongoing desire to grow, no matter if it's to get good grades, find a spouse, or

receive a promotion. A desire to grow will help you get there. Keep in mind that the proof of a desire to grow is the pursuit of that desire.

4. Self-control is the fourth key characteristic of the right person. The right person has an understanding that he cannot do everything he "feels" like doing. If it were up to most of us, we wouldn't even get out of bed half the time. As you are on that road to becoming the right person, you must gain control of what that person does.

5. The last characteristic is friendliness. It almost sounds too easy, but this characteristic will take you a long way. No one wants to be around unfriendly people. Think about it. If you went to a restaurant and the food was good but your server was a rude, unfriendly jerk, you would probably think twice before making this the "right" restaurant. Remember to keep in mind the importance of being a friendly person.

3 WAYS TO GUARD YOUR THOUGHT LIFE

Protection. We guard our home, car, skin, and even time, but sometimes we neglect to guard one of the most important areas—our thought life. We need to place a guard over our thought life.

Here's how:

1. **Take control.** Don't allow your thoughts to wander like an out-of-control car. Grab hold of the steering wheel. The Word of God says to take captive every thought and to bring it into the obedience of Christ. (2 Cor. 10:5.) You may not be able to control every thought that comes in, but you can determine whether or not it stays.

2. **Guard your gate.** What's the gate of your mind? It's your eyes and ears. Don't put junk into your thought life by throwing open the gate. Filter what comes in. Remember the computer term G.I.G.O.: garbage in, garbage out.

3. **Thought replacement.** When thoughts of fear or doubt come your way, replace them with love and faith.

You cannot have 2 complete thoughts in your mind at the same time. For good thought replacement ideas, see Philippians 4:8.

3 STRATEGIES TO CONQUER PEER PRESSURE

Satan wants you to lose. His plan is for you to be the wrong person, not the right person. One of his most common tactics is using people around us to influence us in a negative way. That negative influence is what we call peer pressure. The good news is that we can implement 3 practical strategies to conquer peer pressure.

1. **Have good friends.** If you have friends who don't compromise in their Christian beliefs, it will help you to do the same. First of all, they won't ask you to do things they believe are morally wrong. Second, they will help you be accountable for your actions.

2. **Have a predetermined reaction.** In other words, know how you would respond in a particular situation. How would you react if someone tried to influence you in a negative way? It's a lot easier to respond when you already have your mind made up.

3. **Avoid compromising situations.** If you are trying to lose weight, the last place you want to get a job is the chocolate factory. The best way to conquer peer pressure is to avoid it as much as possible.

6 QUESTIONS YOU MUST ANSWER RIGHT

Questions are everywhere–from your little brother to your final exams at school. Without questions we couldn't have answers. Questions help to bring about truth.

If you want to be the right person, you must answer the following questions right.

1. If I were to ask Jesus, "Should I be doing this," would He say yes?

2. Are my actions and words affecting my future and the future of my loved ones in a positive way?

3. If my thought life were to be shown at the local movie theatre, would I invite my parents to watch?

4. If my actions and words were broadcast on the 5:00 news, would I be embarrassed?

5. Have I spent quality time with God today?

6. Is this relationship in my life helping me or hindering me?

4 DANGER ZONES IN
MODERN ENTERTAINMENT

I enjoy good entertainment just as much as the next guy, but I believe that we all must guard the gates of our minds and hearts. Second Timothy 3:1-6 says we are to have nothing to do with wicked and ungodly people. This biblical principle also applies to our entertainment.

Here are 4 danger zones that we must steer clear of in modern entertainment.

1. **Sexual immorality.** The Word of God says that there should not even be a hint of sexual immorality in our lives. (Eph. 5:3.) Have the courage not to compromise even when everyone else will.

2. **Disrespect for authority.** Honoring and obeying our parents will bring us blessings. (Ex. 20:12.) Paul wrote that our police, military, and government leaders are ministers of God. (Rom. 13:6.)

3. **Mocking of God.** Did you know that when you fail to react to others' degrading of God and godly principles, you come into agreement with those acts? Jesus said

that if you're ashamed of Him and the Word, He will be ashamed of you. (Luke 9:26.)

4. **Rage.** Don't believe that uncontrolled anger will bring a solution to your problem. It won't. It will add to your already existing problems. Proverbs 14:16 NIV says, "A fool is hotheaded and reckless." Don't be a fool.

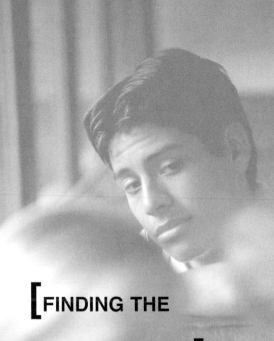

[FINDING THE

RIGHT PERSON]

4 REASONS NOT TO TRY TOO HARD

There are times when you can try too hard to get something you really want. I have seen this more often in relationships than in any other area. We must learn to be patient for God's plan for our lives to develop in His timetable, not ours.

Here are 3 reasons not to try too hard to find the one you're looking for.

1. **Trying too hard and pushing too fast will result in a relationship with the wrong person.** Often, if you're trying too hard, you take the first person who comes along.

2. **Others will perceive you as desperate.** This will naturally repel people from you, and you may miss God's best.

3. **Trying too hard shows a lack of faith in God.** Hebrews 11:6 says that we can't please God without faith and faith believes God will reward those who diligently seek Him. Don't seek after relationships. Seek God, and the right relationships will come.

4. **You can go broke.** If you become a "serial dater," you're going to take a major hit in your wallet, especially if you're a guy. This may be a bit on the practical side, but it's still true.

5 KEYS TO KEEP CHRIST FIRST

If we seek to save our lives, we will lose them; but if we lose our lives for Christ's sake, we will find them. (Luke 17:33.) This is somewhat of a paradox, but it is absolutely the truth. It's only when we truly allow Jesus to take all the controls of our lives that things will really take off in the right direction.

Here are 5 keys to keeping Christ first.

1. **Fill your mind with good, life-giving information.** The Bible, good books, and edifying music are just some of the things that can help keep your focus on the Lord.

2. **Pray regularly.** Make God your best friend, not the heavenly rescue team that you only call on when you're in trouble.

3. **Keep good Christian friends.** Proverbs 13:20 says that the companion of fools will be destroyed. Avoid the fools.

4. **Stay committed to your local church.** Christians are unable to survive alone. We are called to be

connected to the Body of Christ in a local church. Go every week, and get involved.

5. **Get rid of sin and weights.** Hebrews 12:1 teaches us that if we want to finish the race God has called us to run, we must lay aside our sin and the weights that may hold us back. You know if there's something holding you back. Leave it behind.

4 DANGER SIGNS TO WATCH FOR IN THE WRONG PERSON

The Bible warns us not to be unequally yoked together with unbelievers. (2 Cor. 6:14.) The word "yoke" means to be bound together in commitment to one another. When 2 animals are yoked together, when one turns left, the other has to turn left too. It is critical that you walk with people who are going in the right direction.

Here are some flashing warning signs that you may be hanging out with the wrong person.

1. Your conversation always turns away from spiritual things. Those who are really living for Christ will not be ashamed to talk about it.

2. The person is not clear on his or her standards and convictions. If you are with someone who never seems to have an opinion on what is right or what is wrong—DANGER.

3. All of the person's other friends seem to be people who compromise and are not really serving God. This is a dead giveaway that the person is heading down a different road than you want to be on.

4. The person's claim to "believe in God" rarely produces any actions to back it up. The Bible says even the devil believes in God (James 2:19)—so obviously "just believing" is not enough.

7 CRUCIAL QUALITIES YOU MUST FIND

Proverbs 31:10 NKJV asks the question "Who can find a virtuous wife [or husband, for that matter]? For her [or his] worth is far above rubies." This statement confirms the fact that if you are going to find the right person, you are going to have to look very hard to find virtuous qualities.

Here are 7 characteristics you must put on the top of your list.

1. **The person must be born again.** It is not enough to go to church; a virtuous person really is saved and serving God.

2. **The person must have a commitment to sexual purity.** They must have had this commitment before you showed up—not *because* you showed up.

3. **The person must be truthful and honest.** If a person lies to you about small things, he or she will lie to you about the big things one day.

4. **The person must be able to control his or her tongue.** If slander, gossip, or foul language are a normal part of a person's vocabulary, back off.

5. **The person must honor authority.** (Isa. 1:19.) A person who has a rebellious attitude towards those in leadership is headed for destruction.

6. **The person must hate sin.** Proverbs 8:13 says to fear God and hate evil. Does this person?

7. **The person must respect you.** Does this person treat you with dignity, purity, honor, and respect? If not, move on.

3 THINGS THEY DON'T TELL
YOU ABOUT EVERY PERSON

In your quest to find Mr. or Mrs. Right, I've got a flashing piece of revelation for you. You're never going to find someone who is perfect in all he or she does. What you want to find is someone who has a "perfect heart." A perfect heart will quickly make changes and adjustments after sinning or making mistakes.

Locate someone with a heart after God and remember these 3 things.

1. Every person has certain "personality quirks" that may rub you the wrong way sometimes. Maybe he or she is not really organized or takes forever to make a point when talking. Work with the person.

2. Every person is going to find some things in you that he or she doesn't like. In fact, God will use other people to help sand down your rough edges and make you a better person. Be willing to learn.

3. Every person is going to have days when he is not really handsome or she is not incredibly beautiful. It's

okay to be attracted to someone's good looks, but if your relationship is not built on Christ and character, it will never last.

[LOVE VS. LUST:

WINNING THE BATTLE]

5 SIGNS A RELATIONSHIP IS
CENTERED ON THE LOVE OF GOD

When you first meet someone you are attracted to, there is usually a warm fuzzy feeling inside. Your heart pounds and maybe you even get goose bumps, but these feelings shouldn't be confused for God's love. You may have a "crush" or "puppy love." However, God's love is much deeper and more sincere.

Here are 5 signs to tell if you are in God's love.

1. You love the other person for who he or she is rather than what you get from the person. God freely gave us His Son with no strings attached. (John 3:16.)

2. You have Christ at the center of your relationship. (Matt. 6:33.) When Jesus is at the center of all you do, your conduct will never bring you shame or regret.

3. You are waiting until marriage for any physical relationship. Love is patient and willing to do what is right before God and best for the relationship. (1 Cor. 13:4.)

4. You respect the other person's feelings and wishes. Love never pushes someone to compromise what he or she believes is right. (1 Cor. 13:5.)

5. Love seeks to serve the other person rather than be served. (Phil. 2:3,4.)

Use these 5 benchmarks to measure your relationship to see whether it is built on God's love or human lust.

4 SIGNS A RELATIONSHIP IS LUST-CENTERED

Here are some signs you can look for in your relationships to see if you have strayed from God's kind of love to fleshly lust.

1. You look lustfully at the opposite sex. (Matt. 5:28.) This doesn't mean you can't look at the opposite sex in a decent manner. It's what you are thinking about as you do. If you couldn't look at the opposite sex, you would have to walk with your head down the rest of your life.

2. You're willing to compromise eternal rewards for short-term pleasure. (Heb. 12:16.) Take the path Moses did. He forsook the sinful pleasures of Egypt for the eternal reward from God. (Heb. 11:24,25.) The pleasure of sin lasts only for a season, but the reward of purity lasts forever.

3. You manipulate others to get what you want. "Baby, if you really loved me, you would prove it." If you really loved the person you said that to, you wouldn't ask him or her to compromise God's Word. The proof of love isn't physical; it's obeying God's Word and keeping Him at the center of your relationships.

4. You feel like you have to give in to the other person's pressure because you are afraid he or she won't love you if you don't. Perfect love casts out all fear. (1 John 4:18.) If your love is based on God's Word, you won't fear a human being. You will be more concerned about what God thinks than what anybody else thinks.

If you examine yourself against this checklist and find you are in lust instead of love, follow these steps.

1. Repent. (1 John 1:9.)

3. Renew your mind. (Rom. 12:2.)

4. Rebuild your relationship on God's Word.

4 WAYS TO AVOID SEXUAL TEMPTATION

You have probably seen someone mess up and make the excuse "the devil made me do it." This isn't a scriptural statement, because the devil can't make you do anything. He can only tempt you to sin. (Matt. 4:3.) You have to make the choice. Here are 4 choices you must make to help you avoid sexual temptation.

1. **Avoid the places of temptation.** (Rom. 13:14; 2 Tim. 2:22.) If you are around friends who feed you temptation, get new friends. If certain movies arouse temptation, change what you watch. Don't be alone with the opposite sex where you could be tempted. Stay in public.

2. **Purpose to remain pure.** (Dan. 1:8.) Daniel decided before temptation came that he would obey God's Word. You must decide up front to live pure. If you wait until you are in the middle of temptation, your resolve to do right will be weak.

3. **Hold yourself accountable to someone.** (Heb. 10:25.) Find a good spiritual friend who will encourage you in the things of God. When you know you

have to answer to someone about your actions, it helps you stay on course.

4. **Be full of God's Word.** (Ps. 119:11.) God's Word is your weapon to overcome temptation. Willpower alone isn't enough. Jesus used Scriptures to overcome temptation. (Matt. 4:1-11.) If you put God's Word in your heart before the battle, it will come out in the battle when you need it.

You can overcome sexual temptation if you carefully and diligently follow these practical steps.

7 SCRIPTURES TO ARM
YOUR HEART WITH PURITY

God's Word is called the sword of the spirit. (Eph. 6:17.) This is our main weapon to resist temptation. If you leave your sword at home, it can't help you in the battle in your daily life. The answer is what David did in Psalm 119:11. He put God's Word in his heart so it was there when he needed it. To help you do this, write down these 7 Scripture paraphrases on a 3 x 5 index card and carry it in your pocket. When you get a few moments throughout your day, pull these Scriptures out and memorize them so they will be in your heart when you need them.

1. **2 Timothy 2:22**: Flee youthful lusts.

2. **Ephesians 4:22-24**: Put off your old self; put on the new.

3. **2 Corinthians 5:17**: You are a new creation in Christ.

4. **Job 31:1**: Be careful what you watch.

5. **2 Peter 1:3**: He has given you everything you need. (You have a "need" for purity.)

6. **2 Corinthians 10:5**: Take every thought captive.

7. **Romans 13:14**: Make no provision for the flesh.

These Scriptures will help you walk in victory. Just as Jesus used Scripture to resist temptation and overcome, so can you. (Luke 4:1-13.)

3 IMPORTANT STEPS TO TAKE
IF YOU'VE SINNED SEXUALLY

If you have sinned sexually, it's important to realize that God isn't mad at you. Read the story in John 8:1-11 about how Jesus responded to the woman caught in adultery. He didn't condemn her. He forgave her and told her to go and sin no more. Don't be afraid to go to God like Adam and Eve, who hid from Him in the Garden. (Gen. 3:8.)

Here are 3 steps to help you get back on your feet if you have sinned sexually.

1. **Repent.** (1 John 1:9.) This means to do a 180-degree turn from the direction you were going. Notice, this verse says He will forgive and cleanse you.

2. **Reject condemnation from the devil.** The Holy Spirit never condemns; He only convicts. Condemnation is a feeling of hopelessness. Conviction is a stirring to repent and move forward in God. (Rom. 8:1-4.)

3. **Restore yourself spiritually by seeking godly counsel.** Find a spiritual leader in your life, such as a

parent, youth pastor, or youth leader you can confide in and receive godly counsel and encouragement from. (James 5:16; Prov. 28:13.)

Put these steps into practice, and you will be on course to recovery and to even greater spiritual heights than before.

[HAPPILY EVER AFTER]

5 REASONS TO MAINTAIN SEXUAL PURITY
BEFORE MARRIAGE

The Bible instructs us to live a life free from sexual immorality. (Eph. 5:3; Col. 3:5; 1 Thess. 4:3.) However, God isn't trying to rob you of fun and pleasure. He has your best interest at heart. In fact, God created sex for our enjoyment as long as it is in the boundaries of marriage. (Heb. 13:4.)

Here are some of the reasons God instructed us to remain sexually pure before marriage.

1. **God protects us from a broken heart.** When you give yourself to someone sexually, you are giving that person your heart as well. If this person is not your spouse, then part of your emotions are in the hands of someone else. (1 Cor. 6:16.)

2. **God protects you from sexually transmitted disease and possible premature death.** (Rom. 1:27.) Every day young people die from AIDS. Not any of them ever thought it would happen to them.

3. **God protects your marriage from emotional baggage from the past.** You can be married to your spouse and have no guilt from past mistakes.

4. **God also helps you protect your self-esteem.**

5. **You are worth the wait.** If someone says he or she loves you but won't wait until marriage to have sex, then that person is lying. Love is patient. (1 Cor. 13:4.) You are worth waiting for.

Resist the temptation to give in to sexual pressure. God has your best in mind.

4 THINGS TO LOOK FOR IN A GREAT HUSBAND

Ladies, before you start thinking about marriage, you should know what is important to look for in a man. If you were shopping for a car, you wouldn't just buy the first one a salesperson pitched you. You would make sure it had the features you wanted. It's the same thing when looking at a relationship. You should know what is important. Just because a car looks great on the outside doesn't mean it runs. The same is true with guys. Just because they look good on the outside doesn't mean they have what is most important on the inside.

Here are 4 important things to look for in a potential husband.

1. **A strong spiritual leader.** You need a man who will spiritually lead you and be a pillar of faith and encouragement when life's storms come.

2. **A gentle spirit.** Life is too short to live with someone who is always angry and uptight. You want someone who is tender with words, not harsh.

3. **Deep character.** Ladies, you deserve a man who will love you and be faithful to you all the days of your life.

4. **One who respects you and your feelings.** A good indicator of how a young man will treat his wife is reflected in how he treats his mother. That is the way he will treat you.

Before you look for a husband, know what is really important. There may be more things than what I've listed here. Write them down and use them to measure potential relationships. If the traits are not in the person you really want, why waste your time dating him?

4 THINGS TO LOOK FOR IN A GREAT WIFE

Guys, there are a lot more things than looks to consider when searching for the right wife. The Bible says beauty is fleeting. (Prov. 31:30.) It is also what's *inside* that you must consider when building a relationship with a girl. That's what you will have to spend the rest of your life married to. Read Proverbs 31 for some good ideas on what to look for in a potential wife. Here are 4 good things to look for.

1. **Does she love God?** It is more important to have a wife who loves God than one who merely has passing beauty. I have a beautiful wife who loves God, but the thing I find most attractive about my wife is her love for God.

2. **Does she respect authority?** Look at how she treats her father. That is how she will one day treat her husband.

3. **Is she sexually pure?** You don't want a wife who will break your heart because she runs off with another man. When the honeymoon emotions are over, will she remain pure and devoted to you?

4. **Does she believe in you?** It's important to have a spouse who is supportive of your dreams. Life will throw enough negativity at you. You don't need to go home to a wife who doesn't believe in you.

There are probably more traits you want in a wife. Write them down and look at them when you are considering a potential relationship.

7 AREAS OF PREPARATION YOU MUST COMPLETE BEFORE YOU ARE MARRIED

Here are 7 important, but often overlooked, areas to work on before marriage.

1. **Spiritual stability.** Make a strong spiritual foundation in your life. This foundation will hold your life together through all storms. (Matt. 7:24-27.)

2. **Emotional health.** If you have emotional areas that aren't healthy, such as unforgiveness, unresolved anger, and severe mood swings, take this time before marriage to fix these.

3. **Physical fitness.** This will help you attract the opposite sex. It's true your future spouse should like you for what's inside, but he or she will also have to live with what's outside. Take care of your body, and your body will take care of you.

4. **Financial soundness.** Develop good responsibility with your money. Tithe, give, and save. Guys, women are attracted to someone they feel will be a good provider; it helps them feel secure. Ladies, guys are

frightened by reckless spenders; they are afraid they will never be able to satisfy your cravings for stuff. Be self-controlled and modest with your money.

5. **Maturity.** Be responsible in your actions. If you can't take care of yourself, how can you take care of a spouse and children?

6. **Friendship skills.** Learn to be a good friend. After all, marriage is spending the rest of your life with your best friend.

7. **Solving conflict.** Marriage will have conflicts and disagreements. The couples who last can solve differences with love and respect rather than sharp words and fighting.

Preparation time is never wasted time. The more you sweat in preparation, the less you bleed in battle.

6 HABITS YOU MUST ESTABLISH NOW IF YOU HOPE TO ENJOY A HAPPY MARRIAGE

The habits you form today determine the kind of life you live tomorrow. Someone once said, "First form your habits; then your habits will form you." What do you want to be? Form the habits, and your habit will help you achieve your goal.

If you want to attract a great mate, form these important habits.

1. **Patience.** The ability to be patient with others' faults will reap you the fruit of great friendship. What you sow, you reap. (Gal. 6:7.)

2. **Ability to listen.** This is a very important skill. No one wants to hang around someone who monopolizes every conversation. Ask what others think, and listen to them.

3. **Servanthood.** Marriage is a commitment to give your life to serve another. Learn this now, and it will be much easier when you get married.

4. **Humility.** This is the ability to say, "I was wrong; I'm sorry." Many marriages end in divorce because someone could not admit fault or apologize.

5. **Character.** This is the ability to stick to your commitment even when you don't feel like it. There will be many days when you won't feel like remaining married to your spouse, but character will see you through it.

6. **Love.** Read 1 Corinthians 13 for a good description of what real love is. This is the glue that holds a marriage together.

Form these habits, and you will be destined for a rewarding and fulfilling marriage.

every teenager's
little black book
on reaching your dreams

[DISCOVERY]

3 WAYS TO DISCOVER WHO YOU ARE

Perhaps one of the greatest journeys that you'll ever take is the one that leads you to the discovery of who God created you to be. You have a unique personality and skill set that God has given you. Many young people fail to realize all that God has made them to be. Here are 3 things to remember in this exciting journey.

1. **You will be incomplete without Christ.** Maybe you recall the memorable scene in the Tom Cruise movie "Jerry McGuire" when Tom finds his wife whom he had separated from earlier and says to her, "You complete me." Just as God puts two people together in marriage, you are to be married to Christ. Without that ongoing relationship with Jesus, you will always come up short.

2. **Study carefully what God has said about you.**
The Bible is full of Scriptures that describe the attributes and character that He has for you as a person. The Word of God is like a mirror. (James 1:23.) When you look at it and commit to do it, you take on the character of God.

3. **Talk to family and friends about your unique personality.** Many times other people see things in us that we fail to recognize. You may be a great organizer, counselor, leader, giver, creator, or helper, and people around you will see that more quickly than you most of the time.

4 WAYS TO DISCOVER WHAT YOU CAN DO

Proverbs 18:16 promises, "A man's gift makes room for him, and brings him before great men." Believe it or not, God has put special gifts of ability in your life. Here are 4 ways you can find out what they are.

1. **Seek God in prayer, asking Him to reveal your abilities.** Jeremiah 33:3 tells us when we call upon Him, He'll show us things to come.

2. **Ask people close to you.** Solicit the evaluation of friends, parents, teachers, coaches, and others you trust to give their observations on your gifting.

3. **Go after things you have in your heart.** Never be afraid to step out and attempt something you've never done.

4. **Faithfully do the little things you are asked to do, the things you don't like as much.** God promises to give you bigger things when we do the small stuff well. (Matt. 25:23.)

---

7 ABSOLUTES OF GOD'S WILL FOR YOUR LIFE

Have you ever heard someone say, "God moves in mysterious ways"? I sure am glad that statement isn't true. The will of God doesn't have to be mysterious. Here are 7 things you can absolutely count on.

1. **God's will is salvation.** Our heavenly Father desires that all of humankind have eternal life with Him. That includes you.

2. **God's will is dominion.** Dominion simply means control. God wants you to apply His Word and take control of your body, thought life, attitude, and future.

3. **God's will is discipleship.** We are to grow in our walk with Christ. As we mature we are to help others do the same.

4. **God's will is unity.** Your words and actions must be united with God's Word.

5. **God's will is stewardship.** We are to take proper care of our time, money, abilities, and all God has entrusted us with.

6. **God's will is relationships.** Through the power of relationships, you will be able to accomplish things that would be impossible if you were alone.

7. **God's will is progressive.** God has a plan for your life that will be completed one step at a time, not in leaps or bounds.

4 THINGS TO LOOK FOR IN A MENTOR

A mentor is critical in the life of every successful person. Joshua had Moses. Elisha had Elijah. The disciples had Jesus. Oftentimes, mentors won't seek you out—you'll have to find them. Here are 4 clues in finding the right one for you.

1. **A good track record.** Look for someone that has a good history of success in the thing you want to do.

2. **Mutual benefit.** Every great relationship will be good for both people. It is never one-sided. What can you do to help this potential mentor, bringing benefit to them?

3. **Unforced relationship.** Allow the mentoring relationship to develop naturally. Don't try to force

someone into this. Just find a way to be around them by serving, helping, and contributing any way you can.

4. **Ask the right questions at the right time.** Don't overwhelm this person to the point they want to avoid you. Be sensitive to the right opportunities to learn. Most of the time, you'll learn more by observing them.

7 SCRIPTURES TO GUIDE YOUR FUTURE

Can you imagine going into an uncharted forest without any map or compass? You might be lost for years. Many young people are living lost lives because they have thrown down the compass of the Word of God. Memorize these Scriptures. Pray them over your future and let them guide you.

1. **Jeremiah 29:11:** "For I know the thoughts that I think toward you, says the Lord, thoughts of peace and not of evil, to give you a future and a hope."

2. **Jeremiah 33:3:** "Call to Me, and I will answer you, and show you great and mighty things, which you do not know."

3. **Joshua 1:8:** "This Book of the Law shall not depart from your mouth, but you shall meditate in it day and

night, that you may observe to do according to all that is written in it. For then you will make your way prosperous, and then you will have good success."

4. **Proverbs 18:16:** "A man's gift makes room for him, and brings him before great men."

5. **Ephesians 3:20:** "Now to Him who is able to do exceedingly abundantly above all that we ask or think, according to the power that works in us."

6. **2 Timothy 1:9:** "Who has saved us and called us with a holy calling, not according to our works, but according to His own purpose and grace which was given to us in Christ Jesus before time began."

7. **Ephesians 5:15:** "See then that you walk circumspectly, not as fools but as wise."

[INSPIRATION]

3 THINGS TO DO WHEN YOU'RE FEELING LOW

Feelings come and go. We don't have the power to stop feelings of discouragement, worry, or depression from coming. But, we do have the power through Christ to overcome those feelings and move forward in life. Here's how.

1. **Memorize 3 good Scriptures that you can quote out loud to yourself.** Romans 10:17 says our faith comes on strong by hearing the Word of God! Three Scriptures I like to quote regularly are 1 John 4:4, Romans 8:31, and Ephesians 3:20.

2. **Put on some inspirational music.** We all have different music that inspires us and lifts our spirits, but I believe the very best is worship music because it is filled with the Word of God and helps your spirit commune directly with His.

3. **Get your mind and body active.** Someone once said, "Idle time is the devil's workshop." One of the tools in that workshop is the thought of discouragement. When you're active, your mind is focused on the task at hand.

3 THOUGHTS TO ELIMINATE FROM
YOUR THINKING

The Bible teaches us in 2 Corinthians 10:5 to cast down every high thought that would try to exalt itself against the knowledge of God. The act of casting down must be aggressive and then followed with replacement thoughts that encourage your walk with Christ. Guard carefully against these thoughts.

1. **"No one cares about you."** This temptation towards self-pity is a lie. People do care, and most importantly, God cares!

2. **"You won't succeed."** You have every reason to be confident if you are walking with God. Philippians 4:13 says you can do all things through Christ who strenghthens you.

3. **"Just give up."** Jesus didn't quit on you. He doesn't have a quitting spirit and He didn't put a quitting spirit in you. Persevere and finish the race!

4 WAYS GOD GIVES YOU DIRECTION

Do you need direction? Good, because God wants to give it to you. The direction of God is not hard to come by. Here are 4 ways He will give it to you.

1. **The Word (Bible):** the most practical way that God gives you direction. All other ways must line up with this way.

2. **Peace:** how God will lead you. His peace will be deep down inside letting you know you're headed in the right direction.

3. **People:** pastors, teachers, parents, and friends. God will speak through these people whom he has strategically placed in your life.

4. **Desires:** what you want to do. Do you like making art, building, or helping others? God has placed desires in your heart to help give you direction.

3 SECRETS TO BEING INSPIRED EVERY DAY

Inspiration in our lives can come from a variety of places. God has a wonderful way of using different things to get us moving in the right direction. Here are 3 secrets that inspire me in my day-to-day work and relationship with Him.

1. **The power of music.** Although my sons will tell you that my radio is usually tuned into sports-talk stations, I have learned to let music inspire me on a fairly regular basis. Whether it's a great new worship CD or just a song that stirs the soul, music has a unique way of lifting you up.

2. **The power of a book.** What you are doing right now is incredible. Congratulations! You are one of the few Americans that have taken time today to read a book. Of course, the Bible is different from all other books

and should be in our regular reading, but other books also have the power to launch us forward.

3. **The power of people.** The *right* people, that is. Like the pastor of my church each week when he preaches, or my colleagues in ministry who push me to new heights in my career, or my parents, my best friends, and my own family who help me take new ground every day.

3 KEYS TO MOTIVATING YOURSELF
TO DO DIFFICULT THINGS

The easy things come easy, don't they? It's easy to be motivated to play our favorite sport, shop at our favorite store, or eat our favorite dessert. But how do we motivate ourselves to do the hard things like the day-to-day work at school or home, regular exercise, eating right, or any activity that you know you should do, but everything inside of you says "No"? Here are 3 keys I've picked up along the way to motivate myself.

1. **Just start.** There is something magical about forcing yourself to "turn the ignition key" and get things going. It will give you that little bit of momentum to get rolling in the right direction. Make yourself start!

2. **Keep the end result in mind.** The Bible says in Proverbs 29:18 (KJV), "Where there is no vision, the people perish." If you don't remind yourself why you're working, exercising, praying, reading, etc., it will become too easy to quit. Motivate yourself with a vision of what this activity is going to accomplish.

3. **Reward yourself.** Create some kind of reward that you are going to give yourself for completing this task or activity. If might be watching your favorite show, getting a smoothie, taking a nap, or something else you like to do. God rewards us for doing right, so why not reward yourself!

[PLANNING]

3 PROBLEMS OF THOSE WHO DON'T PLAN

Planning is one of the great secrets of success in any area of life. The great thing is this: the God we serve already knows how the future is going to look so He can help us plan better than anyone else. Sadly, there are people who try to "wing it" in life. Here are 3 problems awaiting those who fail to plan.

1. **You are setting up a life system for failure.**
    You've probably heard the old saying, "Those who fail to plan, plan to fail." A lack of planning is actually a game plan to lose in life. Unprepared people are always unsuccessful people.

2. **You'll never inspire others to follow you.**
    People are afraid to walk in the dark. Ultimately, you are going to want people to help you get where you want to go. When people fail to see a plan for where

you are going to take them, they are most likely not going to sign up for the ride.

3. **You'll give up more easily.** A plan gives you the approval you need to reach your goals and a definite finish line. A visual finish line will help you give 100% towards getting to where you want to go.

4 STEPS TO A PLAN THAT WORKS

The Bible tells us in Psalm 37:23 that the steps of the righteous are ordered of the Lord. A good plan isn't accomplished
in just 1 or 2 huge leaps that get you there quickly. It is going
to take time and it is going to take multiple steps. Here are
4 steps that are necessary for a successful plan.

1. **Write down your goals.** You cannot develop a plan
    when you haven't clearly established what you are
    trying to accomplish. It's got to be more than "I want a
    job." What kind of job do you want? What hours do
    you want to work? What kind of skills do you have?
    What work environment are you looking for? Be clear
    about your goals.

2. **Consult with people who have been where you
    want to go.** This may involve taking a person to lunch

or visiting them at their workplace. Perhaps you'll have to read a book or attend a seminar. Get the information you can on their journey to achieve success.

3. **Put together the resources to make your plan happen.** It may mean saving money, buying a weight set to train so you will make the football or soccer team, or simply writing down each resource and tool you'll need and figuring out how you are going to get them and use them.

4. **Be realistic on the time line.** We often try to bring our grandest plans to pass too quickly. Give your plan the time it needs and don't quit until you get there.

8 GOALS TO REACH BEFORE YOU'RE 18

At every stage in life, it is important to learn to set incremental

goals towards the fulfillment of your dreams and vision. I

encourage you to write down your goals as a regular reference

point for your progress. Here are 8 goals to consider attaining

before you're 18.

1. Make a long-term financial investment in the stock market.

2. Read the Bible through entirely.

3. Hold down one job for at least 6 months—a year
    if possible.

4. Read Dale Carnegie's book *How to Win Friends and
    Influence People.*

5. Obtain a basic idea of what career direction you are going to take, and make the necessary plans for school or training.

6. Develop one strong friendship that you will keep for life, no matter where you both end up.

7. Save enough money to buy a decent used car.

8. Keep your grades up, and get your high school diploma.

3 KEYS TO FORECASTING THE FUTURE

Your plan is always an experiment with the future. A good plan that has any hope of being fulfilled must have accurate forecasting of the future. What field of work will be most valuable to you and others in ten years? What is the next big idea in your area of expertise or interest? If you'll follow these 3 keys, the Lord will help guide you into a successful future others may find dim.

1. **Spend time daily in prayer.** Jeremiah 33:3 promises that if we call upon the Lord, He will answer us and *show us* things to come.

2. **Remember that history repeats itself.** A careful study of history will help us properly anticipate the future. In the early 1900s, people were calling for the U.S. Patent Office to be closed since everything had

already been invented and it was unlikely anything new or helpful would come along! This was before airplanes, computers, television, and a million other things. The lesson of this piece of history is to never close your mind to the possibility of change—in any area.

3. **Two heads are better than one.** I've found that I forecast better when I knock heads with my colleagues or coworkers. Challenge each other to dream and think outside the box called "today."

4 SCRIPTURES TO PRAY OVER YOUR PLAN

I believe it is very important to pray the right things over the plan that we make. The Word of God tells us in Proverbs 16:9, "A man's heart plans his way, but the Lord directs his steps." We need to take the time to devise a plan, but as we pray God will direct each and every step to get there. Oftentimes these steps aren't even in our original plan set forth. Here are 4 Scriptures I pray over all my plans.

1. **Mark 11:24:** "Therefore I say to you, whatever things you ask when you pray, believe that you receive them, and you will have them." Believe that you receive your desired goal by faith.

2. **Psalm 37:4:** "Delight yourself also in the Lord, and He shall give you the desires of your heart." Delight yourself in the Lord daily and your desires will be granted.

3. **Proverbs 21:5:** "The plans of the diligent lead surely to plenty, but those of everyone who is hasty, surely to poverty." With diligent work your plan will make you rich.

4. **Galatians 6:9:** "And let us not grow weary while doing good, for in due season we shall reap if we do not lose heart." Have a persevering spirit, knowing that you will reap if you don't give up.

[SWEAT]

4 WAYS TO GET HARD WORK DONE
MORE QUICKLY

Very few of us actually enjoy hard work. That's why it's called "hard work"—because it's hard. The harder the job, the more likely people are to put it off. The longer it is put off, the harder it usually becomes to complete. Just because it's hard doesn't mean that it is not worth doing or worth doing well. Here are 4 ways to get the hard work done more quickly.

1. **Break down the job into steps.** Making the big job several smaller jobs will help you see the progress along the way. Breaking it down will also help you decide how long it will take and what you will need to accomplish the task. Taking a small amount of time at the front will save you time in the long run.

2. **Start right away.** Procrastination only makes the work much more agonizing once you start. Don't let yourself think about how much you dislike the task, or what you would rather be doing. Just start somewhere; you can't finish something that you never begin.

3. **Find out if there is a better way.** Don't just search for a faster way to work; look for the best way. Doing things the right way will always save you time. Cutting corners may seem to help speed things up, but you don't have to re-do something that was done correctly the first time. It is always a good idea to look for the latest and smartest ways to do a job. Sometimes there may be a better tool or technique that could help you finish faster and end up doing a better job too.

4. **Recruit help when appropriate.** If a job is your responsibility, or if you are expected to complete the

work, do it yourself. If you can have help and the help is available, use it. Don't be so proud that you waste time on something that could have been done in half the time if you would have let others help.

3 REASONS "WORKING HARD"
LEVELS THE PLAYING FIELD

There is no substitute for hard work. Working hard will open doors of opportunity that would not have been available otherwise. The greatest achievements do not always belong to those who have the highest score, but the people who are willing to work hard accomplish great dreams. Those who are busy working will quickly surpass those who have a head start financially or socially but refuse to combine hard work with lofty ambition. These are 3 reasons why "working hard" levels the playing field.

1. **Talent cannot work hard.** Talent will take you far, but many talented people have failed because they didn't work. Working hard can help make up for a lack of talent and put you in a position to succeed. Even if you are the most talented person in your field of

choice, if you sit still you will get passed by someone who is hustling to make things happen. Talent is like a seed; if it is not active, it cannot grow.

2. **You can't steer a parked car.** If you try to turn left in a car that is parked, you won't get very far. In order to make choices and navigate through life, you need to be moving. Working hard, no matter where you are, ensures that you are in motion and able to choose the right path. (Prov. 12:24.)

3. **Hard work makes up for your background.** No matter where you came from or what kind of family you have, if you are diligent you will be successful. People want to be surrounded by those who are passionate and will work hard to make each endeavor a success. Others will go out of their way to involve you, if you make the choice to be faithful and industrious. Your

willingness to work hard and finish a job will be far

more attractive than your family name. (Prov. 10:26.)

5 QUALITIES OF A VALUABLE EMPLOYEE

I currently have about 20 full-time employees and interns who serve under my direction and leadership. Each one of them is extremely important and valuable in contributing to our youth ministry. Here are the 5 qualities that make workers valuable.

1. **Diligent.** They give you 100 percent of their effort 100 percent of the time.

2. **Smart.** They think as they work, always coming up with better ways to get the job done more effectively.

3. **Faithful.** They take just as much pride in and give as much attention to the small details of their work as they do big things.

4. **Loyal.** They speak well of you, fellow employees, and the organization to others and always seek what is best for the organization.

5. **Productive.** They get results, are careful with the finances, and help the organization grow.

3 REWARDS ONLY FOR THE DILIGENT

How can you keep up your hard work along the way? One of the keys is to keep your eyes focused on the rewards you will receive for the diligent work of your hands. These rewards aren't just for anyone; they are unattainable to the lazy, slothful, and those who hope to coast to their goals. Be diligent.

1. **Promotion and opportunity.** The Bible says that if we are faithful to put our hand to work in the little things that we will be made rulers over much. You'll never get much unless you do the little. (Matt. 25:23.)

2. **Respect and recognition.** Who doesn't want other people to speak highly of you and what you've accomplished? Diligent people will always be highly favored and find a place of honor wherever they go.

3. **Wealth and windows.** Companies and organizations pay good money to people who work hard and work smart. Money always follows a diligent hand and so will windows. Windows are new ventures and ideas you've never seen before that hard work has opened your eyes to.

4 BIBLE VERSES TO HELP YOU WORK BETTER

God's Word has much to say about the way we go about our work. There is a right way and a wrong way to do everything, including the labor of our hands. Here are 4 critical thoughts to remember when we put our hands to a task.

1. **Our work is ultimately for Jesus Christ, not man.** The Word of God says in Ephesians 6:5 that even when our natural boss isn't looking, the Lord sees and inspects all that we do.

2. **Our work must be planned out well.** Proverbs 21:5 says the *plans* of the diligent make you rich, not just being diligent. So make sure you are working smart, using wisdom to get your job done in the most efficient way.

3. **Our work should produce results.** It's not just about producing a few beads of sweat. Make sure you are accomplishing something in what you do. Colossians 1:10 tells us to be fruitful in every good work.

4. **If we don't work, we won't eat.** (2 Thess. 3:10.) Work is an exchange of your valuable time for your bosses', customers', or clients' valuable money. The old saying, "There's no free lunch," is true. Life is an exchange every day. What you put out determines what will come back.

[NETWORKING]

3 SECRETS TO MAKING NEW FRIENDS

Everyone wants to be liked. That is no different in the "work world." People want friends and they want to be friendly, even those who seem a little "stuck up." Networking is really just the process of meeting new people and making new friends. People are your best resource as you work toward your career, so here are 3 secrets that will help you network and make new friends.

1. **Be friendly.** It seems obvious, but many people get so focused on the task in front of them that they miss the people and possible relationships passing them by. Grab each opportunity to build new relationships by doing the small things that make it happen. Say hello, introduce yourself, or simply smile. Make the first effort by showing yourself friendly. (Prov. 18:24.)

2. **Focus on others.** People want to talk about things that matter to them. If you spend 4 hours talking about your last doctor's appointment to someone you just met, don't be surprised if they start avoiding you. Make the effort to find out what they like and focus on things that you have in common.

3. **Do kind things without looking for credit.** The simple principle of sowing and reaping works in friendships too. If you begin to go out of your way to sow into the lives of people, you will begin to reap the kind of friends that you want. (Gal. 6:7.)

4 STEPS TO BUILDING STRONG RELATIONSHIPS WITH THE FRIENDS YOU ALREADY HAVE

Sometimes the hardest relationships to develop are the ones you have for a long time. It can be easy to take them for granted because it seems like those people will simply be there forever. Those people that you are closest to will be the biggest influence on your life, so developing these relationships is critical to your future. Here are 4 steps that you can take to make those relationships stronger.

1. **Be the kind of friend you want.** Sitting around wishing that your friends would treat you better is only going to wear out the couch. Start treating your friends the way you want them to treat you, and you will begin to see them treat you the same way. (Matt. 7:12.)

2. **Ask questions.** Be proactive. Find out how your friends are doing. Ask them about the things that they are involved in. Focus the questions on things you know they talk about, and be prepared to listen or help.

3. **Offer your help when needed.** No one likes to ask for help; offering your assistance will go a long way with your friends. A strong friendship means being ready to lend a hand to the projects and needs of others without making them beg or feel like they owe you a huge debt.

4. **Be an encouragement.** Try to be as supportive as possible of your friend's ideas or ambitions. You don't have to support dangerous or immoral ideas, but when it's within reason, offer your support. Don't be too quick to laugh or criticize, try always to be your friend's biggest cheerleader.

6 STEPS TO FINDING FAVOR
IN THE WORKPLACE

God wants to help you succeed in all your work. Your success in your job and career will be a direct result of your ability to get along with people. One of the coolest things in the world is having a job you love and working with people you really like. Here are 6 steps to get you there.

1. Don't treat your boss one way and everyone else a different way. People will see your hypocrisy and resent you.

2. Never cheat your company or business by stealing. I'm not just talking about their products or supplies; this also includes their time. If you're constantly late to work, taking long breaks, or leaving early, it's like

stealing money out of the cash register, because "Time is money."

3. Don't try to destroy someone at your work in order to get that person's position for yourself. It will eventually backfire, and you'll be out!

4. When someone else does a good job at your work, compliment the person personally and in front of your boss.

5. Never try to take authority or leadership that hasn't been given to you. Just do your job, and stay out of business that isn't yours.

6. Always give 100 percent. If you can give 110 percent, you were never giving 100 percent in the first place!

3 THINGS TO REMEMBER WHEN
YOU DELEGATE A TASK

Delegation is one of the best ways to multiply your effort. It allows you to be in many places, accomplishing many things at the same time. But delegation is not a "self-cleaning appliance." It does not take care of itself. A job that you delegate is not automatically completed. Here are 3 things that you should remember to successfully delegate any task.

1. **Be detailed.** Just because you know what needs to be done to complete the assignment doesn't mean that the person you are delegating the job to will know everything that you do. As you outline the work, be as specific and detailed with your expectations as possible. This will help you save time by avoiding lots of little questions along the way.

2. **Set a deadline.** If you give someone work to do, tell him or her when you want it done. Many people will wait until they absolutely have to start before they begin to work. If you set a deadline, they will know exactly when you expect it to be done, and you will not have to constantly ask them when they will be finished.

3. **Follow up.** If you are not the one doing the actual work, you should set a specific time when you can inspect the project. Checking the progress of a job will help you avoid problems along the way. If you make a habit of inspecting what you delegate, you will ensure that the work is done with the excellence you need.

4 WAYS TO MAKE A RELATIONSHIP "WIN-WIN"

Being involved in a relationship that is one-sided can be incredibly frustrating. You don't want to be constantly giving and giving without receiving anything from that relationship yourself. Every healthy relationship is mutually beneficial; it is good for both sides. These are 4 ways to make every relationship a "win-win."

1. **Start with you.** The best way to ensure that your relationships are not one-sided is to avoid the things that drain your friendships. Make sure that you are not being selfish or self-centered. Begin to look to do things for others before you expect things to be done for you.

2. **Know your limits.** Decide ahead of time what you are willing to do and what you will not. If you know

your limits and what your priorities are, you will avoid getting into situations where you feel that your friends have taken advantage of you.

3. **Be willing to say "no."** Just because you say "no" to certain things, doesn't mean that you are saying "no" to the whole relationship. The sooner you decide that you cannot do everything for everyone, the sooner you can relax and trust that kindly saying "no" will allow you to do the things that are important to you and avoid the things that waste your time.

4. **Be quick to say "yes."** Saying "no" to certain things will help you manage your time, but that doesn't mean that in a healthy relationship you never say "yes." In order to develop a good relationship you must be quick to say "yes" when you are able or when others have a need.

[OPPORTUNITY]

3 SMALL THINGS THAT CREATE
BIG OPPORTUNITIES

Small things make a big difference. Just like you probably don't think about windshield wipers or toilet paper until you need them or you run out, the small things in life often get overlooked in the big picture of day-to-day living. Taking time to pay attention to these 3 small things may help you avoid pitfalls and create big opportunities.

1. **Go the extra mile.** People often miss great opportunities because they only do enough to get by. Make the choice to do the little extra things no matter how many people notice. Do everything with excellence. Try to be the best at what you do, even if you are doing something that seems meaningless. Attention to detail and doing the little extras may be exactly what will open up a big opportunity for you.

2. **Keep your eyes open.** Observation is one of the best tools to success. As you are faithfully doing what you know to do, keep your head up and looking around. Don't get so busy and robotic that you walk right past your greatest success. It may simply be a better way to do what you are already doing, but if you have your head buried in the sand, you will miss many wonderful opportunities.

3. **Never quit.** The only thing you do when you quit is leave that much more victory for everyone else. The greatest achievements have come to those who have hung in the fight the longest. You can't create opportunities by sitting on the bench, so make the choice to keep going, no matter what happens or how many times you get knocked down.

4 KEYS TO MAKING THE MOST
OF A NEW OPPORTUNITY

New things are always exciting, but if you are not careful you
can begin to place too much importance on your new opportunity. Remember, what you are doing is not the end of the
road. Even though you might be really good at what you do,
you have not arrived at the final destination. The best reward
for doing something well is always the opportunity to do
even more. These are 4 keys to making the most of a new
opportunity that will help give you the opportunity to keep
doing more.

1. **Ask questions.** As you step into a new opportunity,
    ask what is expected of your new responsibility. Find
    out what the goals are for the project or organization.
    Ask about deadlines, schedules, and things that you
    will be expected to take care of. Be as detailed as

possible; this will help you avoid the unknown and give you a head start toward making the new opportunity a success.

2. **Learn how the new opportunity operates.**

   Whether it is a new company, project, or just an added responsibility, learn the policies and procedures before you begin. Learn what is accepted and what is considered rude. Find out how to communicate with your boss about what you are working on. Study the guidelines or mission statement, so you can make sure that you are not going in a different direction than what is important to them. Taking the time to find out the culture of the new opportunity will save you embarrassment and confusion while helping you have favor with your supervisors.

3. **Don't try to be the hero.** When you arrive in a new opportunity, it is often because you were considered to be good at what you do. In an environment with new people or just new responsibility, it can be easy to feel like you have to prove yourself to everyone involved. One of the best ways to make the most out of the new opportunity is to relax and be natural. You don't have to save the world overnight. Do your very best at everything you do, and the opportunity to voice ideas and make suggestions will come.

4. **Work hard.** The more opportunity you receive, the more grateful you should become and the harder you should work. Those who stop working when they advance are those who stop advancing. If you want to make the most out of a great opportunity, roll up your sleeves and start working.

5 DECISIONS YOUNG PEOPLE MAKE THAT

SABOTAGE THEIR FUTURE

Who you are now and who you will be is determined by the decisions you make. One out of every one person will make decisions. When you have to make a decision and don't, that is in itself a decision. So the question is, what kind of decision-maker are you going to be? To help keep you from sabotaging your future, here are 5 decisions *not* to make.

1. **Disobey your parents.** God has placed your parents in your life to help guide you.

2. **Make quick decisions.** Before making a decision, take time to think it over.

3. **Develop wrong relationships.** The people you spend time with probably have the most influence on the decisions you make.

4. **Wait for your big break.** You must get off the couch and pursue your God-given destiny.

5. **Give up.** Both winners and losers face challenges, but winners don't quit.

4 OBSTACLES THAT COME WITH
EVERY GREAT OPPORTUNITY

Great opportunities do not come without challenges. Often, the greater the opportunity, the greater the challenge will become. If it were always easy, people would be walking into something new all the time, and you would never hear anyone complain about never getting a break. Preparing now to meet those challenges will keep you from being surprised and give you courage to overcome each one. Here are 4 of the biggest obstacles that come with every opportunity.

1. **Sacrifice.** If people only did the same things that have always been done, we would still be living in caves and using leaves for clothes. Great advancements come when someone is willing to sacrifice, because they are passionate about what was possible. Whether it is time, energy, money, fame, or popularity, as you set your

priorities you will have to sacrifice certain things to make the most out of any great opportunity.

2. **Knowledge.** Many times the full potential of an opportunity is never realized because the people involved simply didn't know enough. That fact has kept many people from trying to accomplish great things. As you undertake any great opportunity, there will be times when you feel like you just don't know enough, but that doesn't mean that you are not the right person for the job. Make the choice now to study and surround yourself with wise people and you will succeed where others have failed, even if you don't always immediately know the answer.

3. **Distraction.** There is so much going on in the world and so many things that try to grab your attention. If you don't choose to stay focused, you will get tripped

up by one of the biggest obstacles to opportunity. Those who can maintain their focus and see vision through to reality are the people who will be able to seize the opportunity and make the most of it.

4. **Fear.** The single biggest obstacle to success of any kind is fear. Fear will cause you to freeze and question if you really can do anything at all. Fear can make you say "what if" instead of "why not." If you allow yourself to look at opportunity through eyes of fear you will watch each opportunity pass you by and miss the great rewards of making a stand. God doesn't want you to react out of fear; He wants you to enjoy all the blessings of moving past that obstacle and making the most out of your opportunities. (2 Tim. 1:7.)

3 MENTAL MISTAKES THAT DENY
YOU OPPORTUNITY

Whether it is a school you want to be admitted to, a job you would love to have, or just a promotion, there are mistakes that you can make that will cost you the opportunity you desire. Many mistakes are obvious, but others are mistakes that people make every day and do not even realize that they are losing opportunities by not thinking through the choices they make. These mistakes are mental mistakes. Here are 3 major mental mistakes that can deny you great opportunity.

1. **Leaving projects un-finished.** Big projects take weeks and even months to complete, but daily tasks should be finished right away. When people constantly have to finish what you start, they will eventually stop trusting you with anything important. No one likes doing your job for you, and "I forgot" will only

work once or twice. Make yourself daily checklists
and think through the little things that may not seem
big to you but show the people around you big things
about your character.

2. **Making choices without permission.** Often,
opportunity will be given based on trust. You can miss
that opportunity if you make choices without going
through the proper chain of command. It can be easy
to forget to ask, and sometimes it may seem like extra
work, but it is a little extra that can go a long way
toward proving that you are trustworthy.

3. **Complaining.** Watch what you say. People complain
and then wonder why they don't get the promotion they
wanted. If your supervisor notices that you complain
about everything, they will think twice about how you
will talk about them when they are not around.

Sometimes it is natural to talk about the things that went wrong or a decision you didn't like, but show loyalty with your words if you want people to trust you.

every teenager's
little black book
of hard to find information

[RELATIONSHIPS]

6 REASONS TO SAY NO TO PREMARITAL SEX

The Bible teaches us in 1 Corinthians 6:18 to flee sexual immorality. God is not a "Grinch" trying to steal all the fun out of your teenage years. He wants to protect you and prepare you for a wonderful marriage relationship where sexuality will have its perfect place.

Here are 6 reasons to say no until then.

1. You will close the door on sin and its destructive nature.

2. The thought of raising a baby while you're a teenager will never enter your mind.

3. You will never have a doctor tell you that you've contracted a sexually transmitted disease.

4. Friends and classmates will never see compromise in your life that will cause them to talk behind your back and lose respect for who you are.

5. God will be able to trust you with His very best as you give Him your very best.

6. You will never have to deal with "ghosts of relationships past" in your marriage relationship.

6 REASONS TO BREAK UP WITH SOMEONE

I discourage you from "going out" or "dating" too early. The Bible has much to say about developing good friendships but nothing about dating. As you grow older and a good friendship develops into a romantic relationship, be careful to keep things on the right track.

In case you're not sure, here are 6 reasons to break off a relationship that has gotten off track.

1. If you are being pressured in any way to take the relationship to a "physical" level, know it is inappropriate.

2. If you are verbally, mentally, or physically abused in any way, get out of the relationship—quickly.

3. If your partner doesn't show the spiritual drive and Christian attributes that you know are necessary to be strong for Christ, it's time to let go.

4. If you feel used in any way for what you have, give, own, or provide, don't stay in the relationship. Be sure the person likes (or loves) you. Period.

5. If you find the person to be a liar, don't stick around. Trust can only be built on truth.

6. If the person breaks up with you, let go. Seriously. There are many fish in the sea, and you may have just gotten rid of "Jaws," so move on!

5 FRIENDS THAT WILL TAKE YOU DOWN

The Bible tells us that those who walk with the wise will be wise, but the companion of fools will be destroyed. (Prov. 13:20.) Here are 5 different kinds of "friends" that can destroy your relationship with the Lord.

1. **The mocker:** the friend who always makes fun of spiritual things.

2. **The doubter:** the friend who believes and talks about the worst; usually the last to acknowledge what God can do.

3. **The compromiser:** the friend who goes to church and talks a good talk but, more often than not, does not back it up with a life that honors God.

4. **The proud:** the friend who thinks he or she is more spiritual than you or anyone else and constantly displays a critical attitude about everyone else's "lack of commitment."

5. **The gossip:** the friend who always "talks down" other people around you. If a person says negative things to

you about his or her other friends, what is the person saying to them about you?

7 WAYS TO AVOID PREMARITAL SEX

It's one thing to know that we should flee sexual immorality, but you may be wondering, "How do I do it?" Here are 7 ways that you can avoid the sin that can destroy you and your future.

1. Sexual sin starts in the mind, so win the war there first by studying the Bible. Fill your mind with God's Word.

2. Stay in church. The more you hear the Word and stay close to other Christians, the better you will keep your focus on spiritual things.

3. Don't ever go out alone with a person you know will tempt you or easily give in to sexual sin.

4. Don't allow yourself to be alone with the opposite sex in a place where temptation is easily fostered.

5. Stay away from sexually suggestive books, magazines, photos, or Web sites that will stir up sexual desires.

6. Build relationships of accountability with parents and strong Christian friends. When going through a trying time, let them know and ask for their help.

7. Make up your mind. Never retreat. Let every new friend you meet know you are committed to sexual purity.

5 QUESTIONS REAL FRIENDS
SHOULD ASK EACH OTHER

A smart person is known by the good questions he or she asks. When Jesus was 12 years old, He was found in the temple asking questions of the teachers of the law.

Here are 5 questions that good friends should ask each other.

1. How can I be a better friend to you?

2. Are there any traits, attitudes, or actions you see in my life that hinder my success?

3. What gifts and characteristics do you recognize as strengths in my life?

4. How can I pray for you at this time in your life?

5. What has God shown you in His Word lately?

[SCHOOL]

4 THINGS TO LEARN AT SCHOOL
THAT NO ONE TEACHES

Make no mistake. Your teachers will give you important information that will prove valuable in the days to come: math, history, science, and trigonometry—okay, at least most of it will be valuable.

There are also some great things you can learn at school that your teachers will not actually show you. Here they are:

1. **Learn the art of discipline.** Take advantage of your free time during or between classes to finish your assignments.

2. **Learn to negotiate.** Develop your skills working with teachers, coaches, and fellow students to "give and take" in order to reach your goals.

3. **Learn to say no.** Classmates will ask you to cheat, lie, gossip, lust, vandalize—you name it. Put no in your vocabulary.

4. **Learn to love without respect of persons.** You will meet people every day who don't appeal to you. Love them with Christ's love in spite of your feelings.

7 KEYS TO REMEMBERING
WHAT YOU STUDIED

When you think of school you may think of "tests." The key to passing is the ability to remember what you learned a long time ago, even if you were only half awake and it was a Monday morning.

So here are some keys to doing just that.

1. Actually listen to the teacher while in the class.

2. Take good notes—even if your mind tells you it has the ability to "remember all things."

3. Talk with a friend or parent later that day about what you learned—even if it's spiced with a tinge of humor.

4. Remind yourself about all the rewards that come with a good grade.

5. When studying, write your key points down again.

6. When studying, say your key points aloud multiple times.

7. Pray and ask God to bring those things you've learned back to your remembrance. (John 14:26.)

5 THINGS YOU'LL WISH YOU'D LEARNED
10 YEARS AFTER GRADUATING

It's been more than 10 years since I got out of high school and jumped into the "real world." Here's what I found out. No matter how bad you thought school was at the time, you will usually only remember the good times. Here are some things you should do before you graduate.

1. **Keep a "highlights" journal.** You don't have to write in it every day—just when cool things happen.

2. **Take lots of pictures or video.** It isn't just for you, but for your kids. The one thing my kids love to ask about is what I was like in high school.

3. **Share your faith in Jesus with your friends.** You may think you'll be friends forever, but you won't. Some move away, others become too busy, some die, and others just drop right out. Seize the day! (2 Cor. 6:2.)

4. **Experiment.** Try out different sports, new hobbies and interests, different classes, fresh challenges. You

may catch on to something great you didn't know existed!

5. **Study hard, and work hard.** The discipline you develop today will bring you the rewards you'll want a decade from now. (2 Tim. 2:15.)

4 WAYS TO MAKE SCHOOL GO BY QUICKLY

Why is it that when you're having fun, time seems to fly by, but when you get to school it seems the clock has stopped or is moving backwards? Simple: when you enjoy something, you don't care how long it takes.

Here are 4 ways to make school more enjoyable.

1. **Set goals for your grades and achievement.** If you have a vision and you focus on getting there, you'll move at a different pace. (Phil. 3:14.)

2. **Create personal competitions in your classes and with your homework.** As you work on each project, motivate yourself with a challenge of some kind. Set yourself up against the clock, your previous grade, or even a fellow student.

3. **Get involved in something at school you can really can look forward to.** It may be sports, a club activity, cheerleading, school council—in short, do something you like.

4. **Go to school each day with a good mental attitude.** Your mind and your decisions control your

emotions. Proverbs 23:7 NKJV says, "As he thinks in his heart, so is he." Decide every day, "This is the day the Lord has made—I will rejoice and be glad in it!" (Ps. 118:24.)

6 STUDENTS CLASSMATES LOVE TO HATE

A big part of enjoying school includes having friends you look forward to seeing every day. The Bible says that a person who wants friends must show oneself friendly. (Prov. 18:24.) Don't allow your attitudes and actions to cause you to be someone the other students hate to be around.

1. **The pity seeker** feels sorry for him- or herself, trying to get the attention and pity of others.

2. **The bragger** talks about him- or herself, what *"I have,"* what *"I can do,"* and what *"I know."*

3. **The loner** isolates him- or herself from others, making it impossible for others to get to know them.

4. **The gossip** always talks bad about others in the school, including those who are supposedly his or her friends.

5. **The roller-coaster** goes up and down emotionally. One minute they are happy and a minute later they are crying.

6. **The bully** constantly demeans and picks one person that they perceive to be weaker than him- or herself.

[SELF ESTEEM]

5 ROADS TO POPULARITY WITHOUT
LOSING YOUR REPUTATION

Everyone wants to be popular. Popularity isn't a bad thing. In fact, Jesus was very popular during much of His ministry. He never compromised His character or morals to gain acceptance. You can become popular by making both bad choices and good ones.

Here are 5 roads to popularity while maintaining your integrity.

1. **Be a kind person.** You will never be short on friends.

2. **When you do something, do it with all your might.** Excellence draws a crowd.

3. **Promote others and their accomplishments, not your own.** God will then be able to exalt you.

4. **Dare to dream big and pray for the seemingly impossible.** People are drawn to those filled with hope and faith.

5. **Stand up for what is right.** Our world today is desperately searching for real heroes.

7 WORDS TO REMOVE FROM
YOUR VOCABULARY

The Bible speaks about the power of words in relationship to your personal self-esteem. It says, "A wholesome tongue is a tree of life" (Prov. 15:4). Your words will bring life if they are good, but destruction if they are not. Here are 7 words you should eliminate from your vocabulary right now.

1. **Can't.** You can do all things through Christ who strengthens you. (Phil 4:13.)

2. **Never.** All things are possible to those who believe. (Mark 9:23.)

3. **Quit.** "Let us not grow weary while doing good, for in due season we shall reap if we do not lose heart" (Gal. 6:9 NKJV).

4. **Depressed.** "Rejoice in the Lord always: and again I say, Rejoice" (Phil. 4:4).

5. **Hate.** The Holy Ghost sheds the love of God abroad in our hearts. (Rom. 5:5.)

6. **Doubt.** "So then faith comes by hearing, and hearing by the Word of God" (Rom 10:17 NKJV).

7. **Broke.** My God shall supply all of your needs by His riches in glory in Christ Jesus. (Phil. 4:19.)

4 FEARS YOU MUST CONQUER EVERY DAY

Fear is the primary tactic of your enemy, the devil. All through the Bible, we are told to "fear not." Fear will immobilize you and stop you from reaching your goals and full potential. You conquer your fears by studying, speaking, and acting on the Bible, God's Word. When you do, you will conquer these 4 kinds of fear every day.

1. **Fear of failure.** This lie tells you God is not strong enough to help you succeed, and it is perhaps the greatest attack of fear.

2. **Fear of the future.** This lie compels you to believe God is unable to see what lies ahead for you and to direct you in every step. (Ps. 37:23.)

3. **Fear of the past.** This haunting deception says that because of where you or your family has come from, God is unable to make everything good today. (2 Cor. 5:17.)

4. **Fear of comparison.** This lie tries to talk you into believing God favors someone else more because that

person appears to be doing better than you are. The enemy wants you to believe God has given up on you.

6 THINGS YOU MUST BELIEVE
ABOUT YOURSELF

You will eventually become a product of what you believe. All great athletes, presidents, pastors, and corporate CEOs arrived where they are because they believed they could before anyone else believed in them.

Here are 6 things you must believe about yourself.

1. I have been given power over the devil. (1 John 4:4.)

2. I have been given power over every circumstance in my life. (Mark 11:23.)

3. I have a strong body that has been healed by the stripes taken on Jesus' back. (Matt. 8:17.)

4. I have the ability to control my mind and cast out evil thoughts. (2 Cor. 10:4,5.)

5. I am poised for success and will not accept any defeat as final. (1 Cor. 15:57.)

6. I hate sin but love all people and have favor everywhere I go. (Prov. 12:2.)

5 HABITS OF HAPPY TEENAGERS

God wants you to be happy and enjoy life. That doesn't mean you will never experience trials or tough times. Here are 5 habits you can develop as a young person that will cause you to keep your joy through even the darkest hours.

1. **Regularly reading and meditating (thinking and pondering) on God's Word**. (Ps. 119:105.) This will energize your joy!

2. **Steadily communing with God.** "Communion" comes from the word "communicate." That's it! Talk to God, praise Him, and give Him your requests and cares.

3. **Vision thinking.** Find out what God has gifted you in. Take time to seek Him for your career and ambitions. Take one step at a time as you grow to get there.

4. **Singing a good song aloud!** God made us to sing. Not all of us sound that good, but it doesn't matter. Find songs and worship music that inspire you for good, and sing! (Ps. 95:1.)

5. **Attending church weekly.** Stay connected to good friends, strong mentors, and caring pastors who will help you stay on track.

[MONEY]

6 CAREERS YOU CAN START IN YOUR TEENS

While your youth is a time to have fun and enjoy life, it is also a time to learn the value of work and ambition. The Bible has much to say about the importance of working diligently.

Here are 6 careers that you can embark on right now.

1. **Newspaper business.** Throw a paper route, and discover the satisfaction of getting a job done early.

2. **Investment broker.** There are companies that will take investment capital of just $50. Learn how the market works, and start investing a little at a time.

3. **Graphic arts.** If you have a bent for drawing and art, offer your assistance to those in need now. I know 14- and 15-year-olds who design logos and Web sites for companies and churches.

4. **Film and video production.** With an inexpensive camera and some software you can be in the "movie" biz. My son began to be paid for his projects when he was just 15 years old.

5. **Lawn care.** If you have a mower and a weed-eater, distribute flyers in your neighborhood and sign accounts to cut and trim grass after school and all summer.

6. **Child care.** Make yourself available to families for quality baby-sitting services. Be a good one, because they are hard to come by!

4 REASONS YOU'LL HAVE MORE
BY GIVING AWAY

Of course, we know that the Bible tells us to give a tithe (one-tenth) of our income to our local church, and offerings after the tithe to worthy causes. (Mal. 3:10,11.) There are at least 4 reasons you'll have more after you give.

1. The Bible teaches that giving is like planting a seed. Every seed produces a huge multiplication of its kind. (2 Cor 9:10.)

2. God promises to open heaven's windows and pour out blessings that you cannot possibly contain. (Mal. 3:10.)

3. Other people are naturally (and supernaturally) compelled to bless those who are unselfish in their giving. (Luke 6:38.)

4. Giving puts your faith in action, and faith is always rewarded abundantly by God. (Heb. 11:6.)

5 INVESTMENTS EVERY TEENAGER
SHOULD MAKE

An investment is something you contribute to without always seeing a quick or immediate return, trusting that its long-term results will be great.

Here are 5 investments you can't afford not to make.

1. **Invest in your church.** The church is the vehicle by which the Gospel can go forth. Commit to tithe right now.

2. **Invest in missions.** Find a person or ministry successfully reaching the lost, and help out by giving or going.

3. **Invest in your financial future.** Open a savings or money market account, and put something in it every month.

4. **Invest in your career.** Find your greatest interest in life (that can make you money), and read books on how to succeed in that area.

5. **Invest in your vocabulary.** Words are powerful. Learn new ones all the time, using them to be a better communicator, negotiator, and salesperson.

6 THINGS YOU'D BETTER KNOW
ABOUT MONEY

The Bible has literally hundreds of passages that discuss the issue of money. Next to God, it may well be the most powerful force in the earth. You had better know these 6 things about money.

1. It is not the root of all evil. Many say it is, but actually the Bible says, "The love of money is the root of all evil" (1 Tim. 6:10). That is a big difference.

2. No, it can't buy you love. It cannot purchase the love every human soul yearns for—the unconditional love of Jesus Christ.

3. You can have money and still be spiritual. The Bible commands Christians who are rich to be generous—not to take a vow of poverty. (1 Tim. 6:17-19.)

4. Money will come to those who work hard and plan carefully. (Prov. 21:5.)

5. Your good name and reputation for integrity are more important than a quick dollar. (Prov. 22:1.)

6. Don't seek money. Seek God and His wisdom. (Matt 6:33.) Solomon asked God for His wisdom, and everything else came to him!

3 THINGS MONEY WILL DO AND
3 THINGS MONEY WON'T DO

Money can make many things happen for you, but there are a few things that it cannot do for you. Learning to distinguish the difference may be one of the most important lessons you could ever learn.

Here are 3 things money can do for you.

1. **It can multiply.** When you learn how to give and receive, buy and sell, invest and grow—money will multiply. (Luke 6:38.)

2. **It can be an instrument of love.** When you use it to help the poor, the needy, or the lost, it becomes God's love in motion.

3. **It can be a testimony.** As God has blessed and provided for you, give Him the glory and others will see God's goodness.

Here are 3 things money can't do for you.

1. **It can't soothe your conscience.** Giving it away will never bring forgiveness of sin or relief of guilt. Only Christ can do that.

2. **It can't replace your work for God.** Every
   Christian is called to actively serve in God's kingdom
   in some way. Just giving in the offering isn't enough.

3. **It can't go to heaven with you.** Don't hoard it.
   Make the best possible use of it while you're here!

[AUTHORITY]

7 THINGS A PARENT LOVES IN A TEENAGER

The Bible tells us that a wise child will make one's father happy, but a foolish child will cause one's mother grief. (Prov. 10:1.) The attitudes and actions you display in your home have a major influence on the happiness of your family.

Here are 7 things you can do to bring joy in your family.

1. Do your chores without someone asking you to do them.

2. Offer to help with something around the house that is not usually your responsibility.

3. Think of a compliment you can give your mom, dad, or both.

4. Ask your parents if there is anything you can do to improve your behavior.

5. When asked to do something, don't procrastinate even a minute—go right to it.

6. If you have a brother or sister, treat your sibling with the same respect that you would want in return.

7. Be polite, thoughtful, and helpful outside of your home, at school, and in other activities.

6 KEYS TO BEING PROMOTED BY YOUR BOSS

No one likes to work at a job without being recognized and even promoted for one's labor. There are reasons why some people seem to climb the ladder of promotion and authority, while others remain on the lowest rung.

Here are 6 keys to your promotion at your work.

1. Always arrive a few minutes early for work and then stay at least a few minutes late.

2. Do not allow personal issues or other relationships at your job to take time or focus away from your work.

3. Never complain about your pay. You agreed to work for that amount, so be grateful!

4. Ask your boss from time to time if there is anything you can do to improve your performance.

5. Work with your head, not just your hands. Think of ways to do your job more effectively.

6. Don't continually badger your boss with requests for promotions or raises. Let your work do the talking,

pray, and trust God; and when the timing is right, ask
to speak to your boss, without being demanding.

5 REGRETS NO TEEN SHOULD EVER LIVE WITH

The world is full of people who look back with regret on their teenage years. They longingly wish they had done things differently. You have the opportunity right now to assure yourself of no regrets.

Here are 5 regrets you don't want to live with the rest of your life.

1. **Moral regrets.** Don't allow yourself to compromise your purity and be remembered forever with the stains of sexual sin. (Rom. 12:1.)

2. **Ministry regrets.** If the Lord is speaking to you about sharing your faith with a classmate, take the opportunity. It may never come again.

3. **Mentor regrets.** Submit yourself to a good pastor and others you trust to mold you and develop you as a leader. Now is your greatest time of learning and personal development.

4. **Maximum regrets.** Never leave yourself wondering what could have happened—in school, athletics,

church, or any other part of life—if you would have given all you had to give to succeed.

5. **Media regrets.** Don't ever allow yourself to look back at your youth as a time when all you did was watch TV, play video games, and go to movies. Do something productive in your life, along with your entertainment.

CCESS]

7 QUESTIONS TO ASK YOUR PARENTS
IN THE NEXT 7 DAYS

Asking questions is a great way to learn and grow. You gain a perspective on areas of your life that you may have never realized. Here are 7 questions to ask your parents in the next 7 days. Look closely and learn as you read each answer.

1. How can I be a better son or daughter?

2. What do you see as my greatest strengths?

3. What do you think are the weaknesses that I must work on?

4. What friends do you see as the best influences in my life?

5. What kind of career could you see me getting into after I graduate?

6. When do I make you most proud?

7. What is the most important thing you've learned in life?

6 THINGS TO KNOW BEFORE YOU
BREAK THE LAW

The Bible says in Romans 13:1-2 that every person should be subject to a governing authority and that our resisting that authority will bring judgment on us. Here are 6 things you should know if you break the law, whether it is exceeding a speed limit or taking something that belongs to someone else.

1. God is bound by His Word to back up those who establish the laws, not you.

2. Even if you are not caught immediately, the consequences will eventually catch up with you.

3. Know what living on the inside of a 4' x 6' prison cell feels like, because that will be your future home.

4. Go down to the local jail and meet the criminals. If you choose to break the law, they could be your best friends.

5. Get a job making 50 cents an hour. That's about what they'll pay you in prison.

6. Realize that smaller violations will s lead you to larger ones. It will beco spiral that is difficult to recover fron

[s

8 GOALS TO REACH BEFORE YOU'RE 18

At every stage in life, it is important to learn to set incremental goals towards the fulfillment of your dreams and vision. I encourage you to write your goals down as a regular reference point for your progress. Here are 8 goals to consider attaining before you're 18.

1. Make a long-term financial investment in the stock market.

2. Read the Bible through entirely.

3. Hold down one job for at least 6 months—a year if possible.

4. Read Dale Carnegie's book *How to Win Friends and Influence People.*

5. Obtain a basic idea of what career direction you are going to take, and make the necessary plans for school or training.

6. Develop one strong friendship that you will keep for life, no matter where you both end up.

7. Save enough money to buy a decent used car.

8. Keep your grades up, and get your high school diploma.

4 SUREFIRE WAYS TO
DISCOVER YOUR TALENTS

Proverbs 18:16 NKJV says, "A man's gift makes room for him, and brings him before great men." The discovery and implementation of your gifts and talents will bring you the success your heart desires.

Here are 4 ways to uncover your talents.

1. Ask those you know and trust what they see as your greatest talents.

2. Pray and ask God to reveal your gifts and talents to you. Jeremiah 33:3 promises that if we call on God, He'll show us hidden things which we don't know about.

3. Follow your heart's desires, and try new things. The results may surprise you.

4. Be faithful in little things you're asked to do, even if they aren't on your list of favorites. God tells us that if we're faithful in small things, we will be rulers over much. (Matt. 25:23.)

7 PERSONAL BELIEFS THAT
WILL ALTER YOUR FUTURE

Without a doubt, the most important thing you can establish in your life right now is what you believe. Your core convictions will separate you from the pack.

Here are 7 beliefs from the Bible that, if acted on, will alter your future for good.

1. I believe I am God's child and He is my Father. (1 John 3:1.)

2. I believe the Holy Spirit leads me in all my decisions. (Rom. 8:14.)

3. I believe I am more than a conqueror in every challenge life brings. (Rom. 8:37.)

4. I believe God is the author of my promotion in every area of life. (Ps. 75:6,7.)

5. I believe that when I pray, God hears me and answers me. (Mark 11:24.)

6. I believe that as I meditate on God's Word, He makes my way prosperous. (Josh. 1:8.)

7. I believe that nothing is impossible because I believe.
   (Mark 9:23.)

prayer of salvation

God loves you—no matter who you are, no matter what your past. God loves you so much that He gave His one and only begotten Son for you. The Bible tells us that "...whoever believes in him shall not perish but have eternal life" (John 3:16 NIV). Jesus laid down His life and rose again so that we could spend eternity with Him in heaven and experience His absolute best on earth. If you would like to receive Jesus into your life, say the following prayer out loud and mean it from your heart.

Heavenly Father, I come to You admitting that I am a sinner. Right now, I choose to turn away from sin, and I ask You to cleanse me of all unrighteousness. I believe that Your Son, Jesus, died on the cross to take away my sins. I also believe that He rose again from the dead so that I might be forgiven of my sins and made righteous through faith in Him. I call upon the name of Jesus Christ to be the Savior and Lord of my life. Jesus, I choose to follow You and ask that You fill me with the power of the Holy Spirit. I declare that right now I am a child of God. I am free from sin and full of the righteousness of God. I am saved in Jesus' name. Amen.

If you prayed this prayer to receive Jesus Christ as your Savior for the first time, please contact us on the web at **www.harrisonhouse.com** to receive a free book.

Or you may write to us at
Harrison House
P.O. Box 35035
Tulsa, Oklahoma 74153

5 GOOD HABITS THAT WILL MAKE YOU A WINNER

1. **Preparation.** "I will do all I must before, so that I can enjoy the results after."

2. **Action.** "I will do what I need to do right now because tomorrow may be too late."

3. **Prayer.** "I realize that my destiny is too great for me to attempt alone. God will be my constant help and source of strength to fulfill my dreams and achieve my destiny."

4. **Character.** "I will live life with honesty and integrity, the kind of attributes that will not just get me to the top, but keep me there."

5. **Discipline.** "I will continue to do what it takes to succeed, even when the excitement has dwindled, the new has worn off, and things become routine."

5 BAD HABITS THAT WILL LABEL YOU A LOSER

Whether in sports, school, or a career, there are decisions that will form habits and cause any person to come out on the losing end most of the time. Success and failure are not mysteries. You can choose either one.

Here are 5 habits to choose to refuse in your life.

1. **Finger pointing.** "It's someone else's fault that I didn't do well—not my own."

2. **Procrastination.** "I'll get to it later when the mood hits me just right and the universe comes into proper alignment."

3. **Unbelief.** "I don't think I was meant to succeed— mediocrity is just in my genes."

4. **Jealousy.** "I don't see why they get everything going their way. They get all the breaks."

5. **Laziness.** "I'm going to do the very least I have to do in order to get this job done. So what if it's not my best?"

endnotes

little black book on sex and dating

[1] Maxwell, John. *The 21 Irrefutable Laws of Leadership.* Nashville: Thomas Nelson, 1998.

little black book of hard to find information

[1] Strong, James, *The New Strong's Exhaustive Concordance of the Bible,* "Greek." Nashville: Thomas Nelson Publishers, 1990, s.v. "communion," entry #2842.

about the author

Blaine Bartel founded Thrive
Communications, an organization
dedicated to serving those who
shape the local church. He is also
currently leading a new church launch in a growing area of
north Dallas.

Bartel was the founding youth pastor and one of the key
strategists in the creation of Oneighty, which has become one
of the most emulated youth ministries in the past decade
reaching 2,500 – 3,000 students weekly under his leadership.
In a tribute to the long term effects and influence of Blaine's
leadership, hundreds of young people that grew up under his
ministry are now serving in full time ministry themselves.

A recognized authority on the topics of youth ministry and
successful parenting, Bartel is a best-selling author with 12
books published in 4 languages, and is the creator of
Thrive—one of the most listened to youth ministry development systems in the country, selling more than 100,000 audio
tapes and cd's worldwide. He is one of the most sought after

speakers in his field; more than one million people from over 40 countries have attended Blaine Bartel's live seminars or speaking engagements.

His work has been featured in major media including "The Washington Post," cbs' "The Early Show," "The 700 Club," "Seventeen" magazine, as well as newspapers, radio programs, and Internet media worldwide.

Bartel's commitment to creating an enduring legacy that will impact the world is surpassed only by his passion for family as a dedicated father of three children and a loving husband to his wife of more than 20 years, Cathy.

To contact Blaine Bartel,

write:

Blaine Bartel

Serving America's Future

P.O. Box 691923

Tulsa, OK 74169

www.blainebartel.com

Please include your prayer requests

and comments when you write.

every teen girl's

little pink book

special gift edition

by cathy bartel

pink is for princess

and being a princess can be a challenge. discover your heavenly Father's hotline for all the answers in friendships, school, family, and life. find the grace to become something great!

every teen girl's little pink book gift collection includes three complete works in one volume: *little pink book, little pink book for girlfriends,* and *little pink book on gab.*

ISBN-10: 1-57794-909-9,
ISBN-13: 978-1-57794-909-1

Available at fine bookstores everywhere or at www.harrisonhouse.com.